The Collapse of the Soviet Union

Look for these and other books in the Lucent
Overview series:

Abortion	Hazardous Waste
Acid Rain	The Holocaust
AIDS	Homeless Children
Alcoholism	Illiteracy
Animal Rights	Immigration
The Beginning of Writing	Ocean Pollution
Cancer	Oil Spills
The Collapse of the Soviet Union	Organ Transplants
Dealing with Death	The Olympic Games
Death Penalty	Ozone
Democracy	Population
Drugs and Sports	Prisons
Drug Trafficking	Rainforests
Eating Disorders	Recycling
Endangered Species	Reunification of Germany
Energy Alternatives	Smoking
Espionage	Space Exploration
Extraterrestrial Life	Special Effects in the Movies
Gangs	Teen Alcoholism
Garbage	Teen Pregnancy
The Greenhouse Effect	Teen Suicide
Gun Control	The UFO Challenge
Hate Groups	The United Nations

The Collapse
of the
Soviet Union

by Brenda J. Smith

WORLD IN CONFLICT

LUCENT Overview Series

LUCENT Overview Series

Many thanks to my editor, Lori Shein, for her unflagging efforts throughout the writing process; to my friend and colleague, Robert A. Kohan, for his invaluable assistance in reviewing the manuscript; and to my husband, Duane, for his unfailing patience, support, and encouragement.

Library of Congress Cataloging-in-Publication Data

Smith, Brenda J., 1946-
   The collapse of the Soviet Union / by Brenda J. Smith
      p.   cm. — (Lucent overview series)
   Includes bibliographical references and index.
   Summary: Discusses the rise of the Soviet Union and its emergence as a superpower, its ultimate fall and the impact of the collapse.
   ISBN 1-56006-142-1 (alk. paper)
   1. Soviet Union—History—Juvenile literature. [1. Soviet Union —History.]   I. Title.   II. Series. Lucent overview series.
DK266.S5537   1994
947—dc20   93-17097
                                                   CIP
                                                    AC

Copyright © 1994 by Lucent Books, Inc.
P.O. Box 289011, San Diego, CA 92198-9011
Printed in the U.S.A.

Contents

Introduction

THROUGHOUT THE HISTORY of humankind, certain events have shaken the foundations of nations and changed the world forever. One of these events was the Russian Revolution of 1917, which put a violent end to centuries-old czarist rule and established the Soviet Union as the world's first Communist state. Another was the Second Russian Revolution, begun in 1985 by Mikhail Gorbachev, which brought the communist experiment to a close. Through this peaceful revolution, Gorbachev intended to save the Communist party and the Soviet Union. But in August 1991, a band of hard-line Communist party members tried to overthrow Gorbachev and bring an end to his reforms. Although the conspirators failed to overthrow him, their actions spelled the end of his actual power and destroyed the Soviet Communist party.

Gorbachev and the conspirators failed to see that the Soviet people had had enough of the Communist party. They were no longer cowed by years of totalitarian rule and had gained a voice at last. And the voice of the people cried out against communism. Once the party was destroyed, the Soviet Union, a giant among nations in the twentieth century, was dealt a death blow. The Communist party had been the cement holding the multinational Soviet Union together. Without it, the

(Opposite page) Banners of the Russian Revolution, 1917. The revolution marked the beginning of the first Communist state.

7

country crumbled and passed into the pages of history books. Indeed, when the Soviet Union fell apart, the entire world order shattered and a new one began.

Division and unity

So far, this new world order has within it a good deal of division. Many different peoples, conquered and controlled by the czarist empire and later the Communist state, are demanding their own nations. Some countries with many different ethnic groups are splintering into tiny pieces, as neighbor turns against neighbor in the name of independence and national self-rule. Yugoslavia is disintegrating amidst war and chaos. Two separate states—a Czech republic and a Slovak republic—have emerged from the country that was Czechoslovakia. Within the former Soviet Union violence rages in Georgia, Moldova, Tajikistan, and between Armenia and Azerbaijan.

To celebrate reunification Germans join hands atop the Berlin Wall, which once separated East and West Berlin.

However, there is unity in the new world order, too. The threat of nuclear war between the United States and the Soviet Union has passed. The high tension and shrill warnings that marked nearly fifty years of cold war between the superpowers have ended. The line that divided the world into two camps—the Communist East and the non-Communist West—has faded. The Berlin Wall has been torn down. The Iron curtain has fallen. Germany, split into two countries at the end of the World War II, has reunited. Eastern Europe and Western Europe are renewing ties after many years of separation. Within the land that was once the mighty Soviet Union, newly independent countries are struggling to find a common ground for solving their many economic, political, and environmental problems. Nations the world over are sending aid to these countries so that their people can build better lives. Many of the new post-Soviet states, eager to take their place in a new, interdependent world, are trying to set up democracies and capitalist economies.

No one knows for sure what will happen in the years to come. This book is the story of the rise and fall of a great but turbulent nation and the struggle for a future without it.

Following the Soviet Union's collapse, a statue of Lenin is removed from the front of a government building in Bucharest, Romania.

1

The Dawn of Communism

FOR FOUR HUNDRED years czars, or emperors, ruled the lands that were to become the Soviet Union. During most of their rule, all power rested in the czars' hands. As time passed, however, new voices—the voices of the people—began to be heard. In the early 1800s, there were scattered uprisings against the czar and the beginnings of a revolutionary movement. This movement, which was largely made up of middle- and upper-class intellectuals, remained small for a long time. Most of the people in Russia were peasants, who worshiped the czar. Gradually, unrest mounted until the cries of the people exploded into a revolution in 1917 that toppled the last czar, Nicholas II, from the throne and ended czarist rule forever. The Russian Revolution was one of the most important in all of history. Almost overnight, Russia changed from a monarchy into the world's first Communist state.

Harsh living conditions

There were a number of reasons for the people's growing discontent. One was the harsh conditions of daily life under the czars. Russia's economy had changed little over the centuries.

(Opposite page) Inspired by the promise of a better life, a Russian peasant spreads communism among his fellow workers.

Unlike western Europe, which had been swept into the modern age by the Industrial Revolution, Russia had few factories. It was still an agricultural country, and 90 percent of Russia's people were peasant-farmers who lived and worked much as their ancestors had during the Middle Ages. For most of the country's history, these peasant-farmers were serfs, meaning they were legally bound to the land and toiled in fields owned by the czar, the nobles, and the church. Families lived in one- or two-room dwellings with only a table and a few benches, used for sitting and sleeping. They ate bread, porridge, a few vegetables, and, if they were lucky, meat once a week.

In the mid-1800s, the czar freed the serfs and divided the land between the peasants and the landowners. The peasants, however, did not really own property themselves. It was held in common by the village, which made payments to the government. Each year, village elders assigned plots to individual peasants to work. Due to the rapid growth in population, there was not enough land to go around. Much of the time, there was not enough to eat, either. The peasants

While western Europe was in the midst of an Industrial Revolution, 90 percent of Russia's people were still peasant-farmers. These peasants toiled in fields owned by the wealthy classes and lived in meager dwellings.

Peasants who fled to the cities in hopes of a better life were often disappointed. A pre-revolution photo taken in a Russian textile mill illustrates the dirty, dangerous conditions that many factory workers endured.

had no modern equipment, and the climate in many areas was not suitable for farming. As a result, crop yields were often low. Many peasants made their way to the cities, where they joined the ranks of factory workers and served as a growing source of discontent into which revolutionaries could tap. The peasants had left the countryside hoping for a better life. But as they soon found out, life in the cities was just about as dismal. Factory workers toiled long hours for low pay in dirty, dangerous conditions. Many families lived in crowded housing nearby. Often, six to ten people ate and slept in a single room.

No voice

Another reason people became discontent was that they had no real voice in their own government. The czars were autocrats, or rulers with total power. No one had ever been allowed to criticize them. For hundreds of years, they had used secret police to strike fear into the hearts of anyone who tried. In Russia's early days, the secret police dressed in black and rode black horses. On each saddle was tied a dog's head and a broom. The dog's head symbolized the job of sniffing out treason; the broom represented the act of sweep-

During a peaceful march toward Nicholas II's Winter Palace, a photographer captures the czar's soldiers suddenly opening fire on demonstrators. Nearly 1,000 people were killed on this day, later called "Bloody Sunday."

ing it away by killing the czar's enemies.

In an effort to bring about change, the people, who still had faith in the czar, tried to enlist his help. On Sunday, January 22, 1905, a huge crowd of workers—100,000 strong—marched peacefully, singing hymns, toward Nicholas II's Winter Palace. They hoped that their "Little Father," as they called him, would grant them reforms that would ease their daily lives. All of a sudden, the shots rang out as the czar's soldiers fired point-blank into the advancing crowd. Nearly 1,000 people dropped to the ground dead or wounded. The priest who led the marchers, Father Gapon, cried out, "There is no God anymore, there is no czar!" Because of the bloodshed, this day became known as Bloody Sunday.

The fatal crisis

After Bloody Sunday, the fever of revolution spread rapidly throughout Russia, but this massacre did not lead directly to the collapse of czarist rule. That moment came twelve years later as Russia endured the agonies brought on by World War I. This war was the final reason for revolution. In World War I, Russia was allied with Great Britain and France against the united powers of Germany, Austria-Hungary, and Italy. The war, however, caught Russia unprepared. With few factories and many unskilled peasants, the country could not supply its army or care for its citizens. What resources Russia had were mismanaged by corrupt and inefficient government officials. Though brave, the soldiers often had no rifles of their own. They pried guns from the hands of dead soldiers in the field. After three years, almost two million Russian soldiers had lost their lives. Another five million were wounded. One Russian general said, "Today . . . the army is drowning in its own blood." In the cities and the countryside, food and fuel shortages left the Russian people cold and starving. Tired of the hardships, they grew angrier and angrier at the czar.

The anger exploded in March 1917, in what became known as the March Revolution. Hundreds of thousands of people gathered in the streets of Petrograd, now called St. Petersburg, demanding bread and an end to the war. For the first time, they were also shouting "Down with

Soldiers fire upon protesters in the courtyard of the Winter Palace in St. Petersburg. Hundreds of thousands of people gathered in St. Petersburg in March 1917, shouting "Down with the czar!" and demanding an end to their country's involvement in World War I.

The German philosopher Karl Marx believed that communism would eliminate class differences, but that it could only be achieved through revolution.

the czar!" Nicholas, who was at the war front trying to rally the soldiers against the German enemy, received the following telegram from a member of his government:

> Situation serious. In the capital anarchy. Government paralyzed. Transport of food and fuel completely disorganized. Public disaffection growing. On the streets chaotic shooting. Army units fire at each other. It is essential at once to entrust a person enjoying the country's confidence with the formation of a new government. There should be no delay. All delay is death.

Nicholas, however, failed to understand the seriousness of the situation. By the time he realized what was happening, it was too late. Nicholas was forced to give up the throne. Later, the czar and his whole family were arrested and shot. But getting rid of the czar did not fix things. A temporary government, set up to run the country until a permanent government could be created, did little to change circumstances in Russia. Citizens continued to riot over food and fuel shortages, and large numbers of Russian soldiers, involved in a war they did not want, deserted their posts at the front.

Lenin and the teachings of Karl Marx

Into this chaos stepped the man who would change Russia dramatically—Vladimir Ilyich Ulyanov, also known as Nikolai Lenin. Lenin believed in the teachings of the German philosopher Karl Marx, who favored a system called communism. This is an economic system in which the people collectively, or as a group, own the means for producing all goods. The means include factories, railroads, machinery, banks, and farmland. Under communism, people give what they can of labor and knowledge and receive what they need of food, shelter, clothing, and medical care.

One reason Marx favored communism was that

he disliked capitalism. Capitalism is an economic system in which private citizens or companies own the means for producing goods. As Marx saw it, capitalism creates two classes of people—workers and owners. The owners profit handsomely from their businesses, while the workers suffer grave hardships, including poor working conditions and low wages, to make the owners rich.

Marx believed that communism would eliminate class differences because all members of society would be both workers and owners. He also thought that communism could be achieved only through revolution and in stages. Capitalism, Marx said, would give way to socialism, a system in which the government owns the means for producing goods. Socialism would, in turn, give way to communism.

Marx believed that the revolution would take place first in a highly industrialized country, such as England, but his strongest following developed in Russia. There, Marx's followers set up the Russian Social Democratic Workers' Party, also called the Social Democrats. Before long, the party split into two groups—the Mensheviks and the Bolsheviks. The Mensheviks felt that Russia needed to become a fully industrialized state with a large working class *before* a revolution could take place. Lenin and the Bolsheviks believed that a revolution could succeed *at once*—if a small group of dedicated Marxists led it.

The Bolshevik Revolution

In the spring of 1917, Lenin, who had been forced to leave the country for suspected revolutionary activities, was smuggled back into Russia by the Germans. The Germans wanted Russia out of the war and knew the Bolsheviks did, too. In Russia, Lenin won the backing of many soldiers, peasants, and workers by calling for "Peace, Land,

Lenin defied a government-imposed exile by returning to Russia in 1917. His call for "Peace, Land, and Bread!" won him immediate support.

Members of the Red Guard (foreground) stand to protect a Bolshevik leader as he speaks to a crowd of thousands.

and Bread!" In late October 1917, Lenin's supporters overthrew the temporary government in what became known as the Bolshevik Revolution. Lenin became the head of the new government. The first thing he did was to sign a peace treaty with Germany and pull Russia out of the war. Now, he was free to fight his enemies at home.

For the next three years, civil war raged across Russia. The Bolsheviks, who were now called Communists, or Reds, were on one side. The anti-Bolsheviks, or Whites, were on the other. The Whites included three main groups: the Mensheviks, landowners (who did not want to lose their land to the peasants), and royalists (who wanted to return to a czarist form of government). The Whites received aid from some of Russia's World War I allies. They wanted Russia back in the war and also feared that if the Communists won, their revolutionary ideas would spread to other countries. In the end, the Reds, who were united and had a new, efficient Red Army, defeated the Whites.

A Communist state

As followers of Marx, the Bolsheviks set about changing the country into a Communist state. First, they set up a centralized government. In this government, the Communist party had complete control. No other political parties were allowed. Although the government held elections, there generally was only one candidate from which to "choose." So average citizens still had no real voice in the government and no way to change things. And like the czars before them, the Communists used the secret police to root out their enemies and to hold on to their power.

Along with setting up a new government, the Communists took steps to set up a planned economy in which the state made all economic decisions, including what and how much to produce. The state took over privately owned factories and farms and did away with private trade. The government distributed goods to state-run stores and set prices low enough for people to afford. The state provided housing, utilities, transportation, and education to the people free of charge or for a small sum. In return for these benefits, everyone was expected to work.

A compromise with Marx's teachings

The transformation to communism did not go smoothly. After three years, the economy was in shambles. Industrial output had fallen dramatically, and food production had also dropped. Peasant-farmers had no reason to grow more food than was needed to feed themselves, because they could not sell the extra food for a good price in the free market. So they began to plant less and to hoard what food they did have rather than selling

Starving Russians stand in line for food in the town of Samara in 1917. Following the transition to communism, the country experienced one of the worst famines in Russian history.

it. Adding to the problems, a spell of bad weather caused the crops to fail. A terrible famine resulted. One young girl in Moscow said:

> The hunger was boundless. . . . My aunt would cut up tiny pieces of bread and say, "Bite off a little and chew it slowly and wash it down with water so you feel like you ate something. That's all you're getting.". . . One time my aunt and uncle brought home a little round sack of sunflower seeds. They'd swapped a dress for them. And so every day I'd spend a couple hours . . . eating seeds until I felt full.

Before long, people from the cities, hungry and desperate, grabbed any weapons they could and went into the countryside to force the peasants to give them food. Lenin encouraged the attacks, hoping to weaken peasant resistance to Communist rule. More than four million people died in the famine. It was one of the worst in Russian history. Desperate to help the Russian economy,

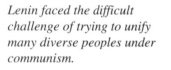

Lenin faced the difficult challenge of trying to unify many diverse peoples under communism.

Lenin was forced to compromise with Marx's teachings. He temporarily allowed the return of a few capitalist practices, including small-scale, privately owned businesses and the sale of produce for a profit.

Creating the U.S.S.R.

The dismal economic situation presented a serious challenge for Lenin, but he faced another even more troubling problem. This was the possible breakup of the new Communist state because of ethnic rivalry. Russia was made up of a patchwork of diverse peoples. Over time, the czars had expanded the country's borders in all directions, conquering many different ethnic groups. These groups had their own histories, languages, religions, and customs but were absorbed into the empire and made to adopt Russian ways. They had to learn to speak the Russian language and to follow the Eastern Orthodox religion. They resented the loss of their own culture and being forced to accept another.

Lenin had hoped to unify all of these different groups under communism and within a federation—a union of individual republics with a central government in Moscow. He established this federation on December 30, 1922, as the Union of Soviet Socialist Republics (U.S.S.R.), also known as the Soviet Union. On the surface, this new union created a nation of one people. But beneath its exterior, the Soviet Union remained a multinational state—a country of countries joined together by force.

2

The Rise of a World Superpower

L ENIN AND THE other Communist leaders knew just how backward their nation was. This was emphasized during World War I, when Russia could neither defend itself nor feed its people. And it was painfully obvious during the country's transformation to communism. There was little industry, unproductive agriculture, and a terribly low standard of living for the people. The new Soviet Union was unprepared to join its neighbors in the modern age. This painful lesson was not lost on Iosif Vissarionovich Dzhugashvili, later known as Joseph Stalin, who became leader of the Soviet Union after Lenin's death in 1924. Stalin was willing to do just about anything—no matter how brutal—to achieve his goal, which was to modernize his country and make it a leading industrial power. It was Stalin's drive and determination that propelled the Soviet Union into the role of a world superpower.

(Opposite page) Beneath giant portraits of Lenin and Stalin, Russian Air Force Academy students celebrate the anniversary of the Russian Revolution. It was the fierce determination of Joseph Stalin that fueled the transformation of the Soviet Union from a backward nation to a world superpower.

The five-year plans

Stalin had a clear idea about how his country could achieve status as a world power. Rapid in-

Stalin moved quickly to achieve his goal of rapid industrialization. He built 1,500 new factories within five years.

dustrialization was the key to his plan. Under policies laid out in what became known as the five-year plans, Stalin began building up heavy industry—steel mills, power and chemical works, automobile plants, airplane factories, and oil refineries. The government converted all existing factories from light to heavy industry and ordered the construction of new plants. Within five years, Stalin's government had built 1,500 new factories. With Stalin's single-minded focus on heavy industry, production of consumer goods, such as clothing and household items, suffered. This meant little improvement in the daily lives of the Soviet people.

The nation's crop-growing regions also played an important part in Stalin's plan to modernize the Soviet Union. To increase agricultural production, he collectivized agriculture, merging small farms to form larger ones. Stalin created two kinds of farms, both of which came under government ownership and control. One was a collective farm, or kolkhoz, on which hundreds of workers joined together to plant and harvest crops. They gave part of the harvest to the government, selling the surplus and splitting the profits after the bills were paid. The workers owned their own houses and a few animals. They were allowed to have small garden plots and could sell whatever fruits and vegetables they did not use. The other was a state farm, or sovkhoz. Even larger than the kolkhoz, it operated more like a factory in which each of the thousands of workers did a certain job and received set wages. The government kept the harvest and any profits, spending some of the money to build apartments nearby for the workers.

Failure and success

Stalin set up farming this way to force anti-Communist peasants to submit to Communist rule and because he believed collectives were more efficient than private farms. The state could,

Russian workers break for lunch on a collective farm, or kolkhoz. Unlike on a state farm, or sovkhoz, workers on collective farms were entitled to share in some of the profits.

for example, provide the collective with costly modern machinery that small farmers could not afford. Under the new system, a particular region could specialize, or produce one product. Then, the government would deliver needed food and goods throughout the country. For example, Kazakhstan grew cotton but depended on the government to deliver fruit from Georgia. Stalin believed that through specialization he would not only have enough to feed the Soviet people, but a surplus to export. And the money earned on exports could be plowed back into industry.

In one sense, Stalin's plans failed dismally. Food shortages and starvation wracked the country, and millions died. The collective farms simply could not produce enough to feed the Soviet Union's rapidly growing urban population. The government made the situation worse by seizing crops for export to foreign countries and by refusing to deliver goods to any farms that did not produce their targeted amount of crops. Lack of good railroads and other means of transportation delayed distribution of food and essential goods.

Stalin's failures in these areas, however, did not deter him from his primary goal, which was to transform the Soviet Union into a great industrial power. At this, he succeeded brilliantly, though success did not come without a price. The cost in misery and human lives was enormous.

A totalitarian state

One reason Stalin was able to force the Soviet Union to modernize and become a great industrial power was that he made the Soviet Union into a totalitarian state. This kind of state has one leader who holds all the power and controls everything. To build and hold onto his power Stalin ruthlessly stamped out all those who spoke out against his harsh policies or who appeared to

Stalin was a tyrannical ruler who stopped at nothing to achieve his goals for the Soviet Union.

threaten the Communist state. The government censored newspapers, books, movies, television programs—everything the people read, heard, or saw. Stalin ordered writers and artists to create only works that glorified him and the Soviet state. Following the Communist policy of atheism, or a belief that there is no God, he closed the churches and the mosques, jailing many religious leaders and worshipers. He uprooted ethnic groups and sent them far from their homelands, making it harder for them to unite and rebel. He slaughtered millions of peasants, because many were staunchly anti-Communist. His secret police watched everyone, striking fear into the hearts of people. Children were taught to watch for traitors to Stalin and communism, and many reported their own parents to the government.

Stalin even turned against members of the Communist party and the Red Army. He removed them from positions of power and then, like all the others he thought were disloyal, had them either shot or sent to labor camps in icy Siberia.

The ruins of a former prison camp, where thousands of anti-Communists died of starvation and disease or were killed by firing squads.

"Even the trees cry"

Zenon Poznyak, an archaeologist, describes Stalin's killing ground at Kuropaty, a forest in Belarus (formerly Byelorussia):

> They shot people here every day. When people were driven to the graves, the pits were already dug. . . . People were taken out of the trucks. Their hands were untied. NKVD [secret police] officers stood around the pits, revolvers ready so that no one could run away. Pairs were led up to the pits and shot in the back of the head. Usually, people, when they were untied, understood that they had been brought here to be killed. They threw themselves on their knees and . . . began to ask why they were being killed and what they were guilty of. . . . They appealed to God, prayed, and remembered their families.

From 1937 to 1941, Stalin had 250,000 people murdered at Kuropaty. For this reason, it is said that "At Kuropaty, even the trees cry." Though records are incomplete, it is believed that Stalin had a hand in the deaths of fifty million people during his years as leader of the Soviet Union.

The Soviet Union vs. the United States

The United States and other Western democracies watched warily as the Soviet Union under Stalin turned to totalitarianism and transformed itself into a leading industrial power. They feared that the Soviet Union might try to expand its territory and its Communist ideas. However, when World War II broke out, the Soviet Union joined the Allied nations led by the United States and Great Britain against Nazi Germany. Though victorious, the Allies experienced difficulties with the postwar settlement.

During the closing months of World War II, the Soviets had liberated much of Eastern Europe from Nazi domination. When the war ended, however, Stalin refused to leave. He wanted to establish Soviet dominance in the new territory. The Allies agreed to the Soviet presence in Eastern Europe in exchange for Stalin's promise to give the countries political freedom. Instead, he used Soviet power to back the formation of Communist governments in the area. Countries such as Poland, Hungary, and Bulgaria became Soviet satellites, which meant that they were controlled by the Soviet Union. In gaining these satellites, Stalin had established an empire.

The Allies felt that an "Iron Curtain" had fallen across the continent of Europe. Although it could not be seen, this Iron Curtain, behind which stood Soviet tanks, was nevertheless a solid barrier that cut off and isolated Communist Eastern Europe from non-Communist Western Europe. Stalin's actions in Eastern Europe triggered a strong anti-Soviet response, especially from the United States. To uphold democracy and prevent the spread of communism into Western Europe, the United States sent millions of dollars to rebuild the war-torn lands there. The United States also joined with eleven other European countries to form the North Atlantic Treaty Organization (NATO). NATO members promised to come to each other's aid in case of Soviet attack. The Soviet Union responded by setting up the Council for Mutual Economic Assistance (COMECON) to help rebuild Eastern Europe and by forming a military alliance called the Warsaw Pact to defend it.

This was the beginning of bipolarism, or the domination of world affairs by two superpowers—the United States and the Soviet Union. After World War II, Europe was in a state of economic collapse and exhausted by war. It could no

Following World War II, rockets were paraded in Moscow in celebration of communism and the Soviet Union's rise as a world superpower.

longer play a leading role on the world stage. The United States, on the other hand, had experienced a time of economic growth as well as great strides in science and technology, including the invention of the atomic bomb. This had strengthened its already leading position among the nations of the world. The Soviet Union had suffered huge losses in the war but had gained an empire and built itself into a major world power.

The two new superpowers soon became locked in a bitter struggle known as the cold war. During this struggle, which lasted for almost fifty years, there was great hostility and tension between the United States and the Soviet Union as each tried to further its influence in the world. It was called a cold war because no actual fighting broke out between the two. Before long, much of the world was divided into two camps—one headed by the Soviet Union in the East and the other headed by the United States in the West. The two countries entered into an arms race and built up huge supplies of weapons—everything from tanks to nuclear missiles. They achieved a balance of power in that both sides were equally strong. But it was really a balance of *terror*, because nuclear weapons made the possibility of all-out war far more dangerous than ever before. Nuclear warfare could easily destroy the whole world.

Khrushchev loosens controls

Stalin died in March 1953, and after a brief power struggle, Nikita Khrushchev took over. Khrushchev hoped to win public support and thus strengthen his own power by loosening the controls a bit. One of the first things Khrushchev did was to attack Stalin, whom he accused of being a cruel murderer. He even had Stalin's embalmed body removed from its honored place next to Lenin in Moscow's Red Square tomb. Although a

Nikita Khrushchev gained public support by attacking many of Stalin's harsh policies.

devoted Communist party member, Khrushchev took steps to change some of Stalin's harsh policies. Khrushchev had many political prisoners released and many labor camps closed. Writers and artists gained some freedom. He gave local managers more control over their farms and factories. Although industrial growth remained a priority, Khrushchev stimulated food production by increasing the number of state farms. He also helped improve the people's daily lives by giving them higher wages and increasing the production of consumer goods. Television sets and automobiles became available to more Soviet citizens than ever before.

While attempting to improve conditions at home, Khrushchev was still trying to maintain the Soviet Union's status as a world superpower. Initially, his approach to the West differed from Stalin's. He believed that in time communism would triumph over capitalism through peaceful competition rather than through force. Toward this end, Khrushchev advanced science and technology in a variety of areas, especially space exploration. In 1957, the Soviet Union launched *Sputnik*, the world's first space satellite. This signaled the beginning of the space race with the United States, an effort by both countries to top the other in an important area of technology.

The Soviet Union launched the world's first space satellite, Sputnik, *in 1957. This event marked the beginning of the space race between the United States and the Soviet Union.*

The Cuban missile crisis

Despite these years of peaceful competition, Khrushchev, like Stalin, ultimately resorted to force to maintain the Soviet Union's world power status. Under Fidel Castro, who rose to power in 1959, Cuba became Communist and formed an alliance with the Soviet Union. Cuba had poor relations with the United States, which was uneasy having a Communist country ninety miles from its shores. The United States also disliked Castro

Khrushchev (right) and Fidel Castro celebrate Cuba's transition to communism and the new alliance between the two countries.

because he sought to spread communism throughout Latin America. Hoping to overthrow the Cuban dictator, the United States, under President John F. Kennedy, backed an invasion of the island in April 1961. The invaders were American-trained, anti-Castro Cuban exiles. The invasion failed, causing the United States to temporarily lose prestige.

The failed invasion also tightened the bond between Cuba and the Soviet Union. Castro called on his Soviet ally to help protect Cuba from the United States. Angered by America's involvement in the plot to overthrow the Cuban dictator, Khrushchev responded by setting up missile bases in Cuba in 1962. By October, the missiles were in place. President Kennedy demanded that the Soviets remove them and stationed American ships in Cuban waters to prevent Soviet ships carrying additional weapons from arriving. As the Soviet ships moved closer and closer to their destination, the world held its breath for fear that the two powers would unleash a nuclear war. Finally, the tension passed when Khrushchev agreed to tear down the bases and take the missiles back to the Soviet Union if the United States would promise not to invade Cuba. Khrushchev's actions, however, caused his ultimate downfall. Many hard-line Communist leaders, who were against his domestic reforms and strongly opposed to the United States, believed that Khrushchev had backed down. They forced him out of power.

The Brezhnev years

The man who benefited most from Khrushchev's fall was Leonid Brezhnev, who ruled the country for the next eighteen years. Brezhnev's philosophy and style of rule was closer to Stalin's than Khrushchev's. He took away the freedoms gained by artists and writers and sent dissidents, meaning people who criticized the government, to mental hospitals or labor camps in Siberia. He again pushed more of the country's resources toward the development of heavy industry, paying less attention to the manufacture of consumer goods. Farms and factories returned to stricter control by the central government in Moscow.

Although there were some periods when cold

Like Stalin, Leonid Brezhnev imposed strict government controls on farms and factories, took away many individual freedoms, and severely punished dissidents.

war tensions relaxed, Brezhnev often forcefully asserted his country's power. He made it clear that he would do whatever was necessary to keep the Soviet satellites in line or to protect Communist gains in other countries. Brezhnev demonstrated his willingness to use force in 1968 when he sent 500,000 Soviet and Warsaw Pact troops to crush a reform movement in Czechoslovakia. In addition, the Soviet Union began a massive buildup of nuclear weapons as well as conventional guns, bombs, and tanks. Like Stalin, Brezhnev felt that the Soviet Union would have a stronger hand in world affairs if it made a name for itself as a great military power. The United States responded with a military buildup of its own. Both nations wanted to make certain that

neither outpaced the other in military might. In 1977, the Soviet Union placed nuclear missiles in Eastern Europe. NATO responded by setting up nuclear missiles in Western Europe in 1979. Growing concern over the possibility of nuclear war led to the start of arms-control agreements between the two nations.

By this time, however, disaster was stalking the Soviet economy. The arms buildup of the previous decades had cost billions. Critical needs in the cities and the countryside had been ignored. The gap between communist ideals and real life was widening, leading to a loss of faith among the Soviet people. Many Soviet citizens realized their nation was in trouble and blamed their leaders. In the book, *The New Russians,* author Hedrick Smith recalls a joke circulating in Soviet cities around that time. The joke reflects the people's dissatisfaction with Soviet leadership:

> A train carrying Stalin, Khrushchev, and Brezhnev stalls somewhere in the [countryside]. The people turn to Stalin, as the senior leader, to ask how to get the train moving. Without hesitation, he gives a characteristic command: "Shoot the engineers. Exile the crew. Get someone new." But a short while later, the train stalls again. This time responsibility falls on Khrushchev, who pardons the crew members exiled by Stalin and puts them back on the job, and the train resumes its journey. . . . It stalls a third time. This time Brezhnev has to deal with the problem. The others turn to him, he thinks a moment, and then orders: "Pull down the shades and pretend we're moving."

As time passed, the pain and suffering of the people stirred up more and more criticism within the Soviet Union and its Eastern European satellites. As economic conditions worsened, unrest mounted. In 1982, Leonid Brezhnev died, leaving many unsolved problems for the leader who took his place.

3

The Second Revolution

DURING THE TWO years and four months after Brezhnev died, the leadership of the Soviet Union changed twice. Then, in March 1985, a new kind of leader took the reins in the Soviet Union. His name was Mikhail Gorbachev. Born into a Russian peasant family, he joined the Communist party in his youth and rose quickly through its ranks. At 54, Gorbachev was the youngest Soviet leader since Stalin. He also was the best educated, with college degrees in law and agriculture. Unlike earlier Soviet leaders, Gorbachev was open and friendly, mixing easily with people on the street as well as with world leaders.

Although he was loyal to the Communist party, Gorbachev was not as rigid about its teachings as earlier Soviet leaders. He felt he could adapt Communist ideas to suit his country's enormous needs. This gave Gorbachev the flexibility to take bold, new steps, which not only attacked Stalin's ways, but shook the very foundations of communism as set forth by Marx and Lenin. The reforms begun by Gorbachev were so sweeping that they have been called the Second Russian Revolution. Peter the Great once said, "Russia is a country in which

(Opposite page) A friendly, more flexible leader, Mikhail Gorbachev undertook reforms so drastic, they are often called the Second Russian Revolution.

Suffering from major food shortages, people were forced to stand in line for hours, often for just a loaf of bread.

things that just don't happen, happen." Gorbachev and his reforms were something that historically "just didn't happen" in the Soviet Union.

Torn by troubles

When Gorbachev took over, the Soviet Union was torn by troubles. The Soviet system had failed, and the economy was decaying from within. For decades, the country had focused on building up its position as a world superpower and largely neglected the needs of the people. Farms and factories were not producing enough, and the standard of living was very low. Store shelves were almost empty, and people had to stand in line for hours to buy food. Consumer goods were in short supply and of poor quality. Most people in cities lived in small apartments that had one or two rooms, with several families sharing the bathroom and the kitchen. In these apartments, there was usually electricity but sometimes no central heating. There was little furniture, and the few pieces a family owned were often old and rickety. Sometimes there was a refrigerator, a television set, or a washing machine, but generally these items were also old. Few families had telephones. People often had to wait up to twenty years just to get an apartment of their own and about the same amount of time to get a car. In the countryside, the peasants often lived in worse conditions. Many of their houses had no indoor plumbing so the family had to use an outhouse and get water from the village well for bathing and washing.

One resident of Moscow, Volodya Konoplanikov, vented his anger about the low standard of living:

> Everyone knows you can't buy anything. . . . There's no point in working. I've put in ten, twelve hours today . . . but . . . I can't buy anything with my money. Everywhere there are shortages—sugar, soap, tea, shoes. Such a great country and it's a real problem to buy shoes. . . . It is to our shame. You know they turn off the hot-water system in Moscow for two months every summer. What are you going to wash in—cold water? This has been going on for the last twenty-five years, ever since they set up a centralized hot-water system.

After years of neglecting the needs of the people, the standard of living in the Soviet Union was appallingly low. Most people lived in tiny, drab apartments with no central heating and few modern conveniences.

In addition to the economy being in shambles, the Soviet system of government had some serious flaws. The country's Communist rulers had turned out to be as autocratic as the czars before them. They controlled the lives of the masses, who felt they had no stake in the Soviet system. As a result, many people cared only about themselves, their families, finding enough food to eat and staying out of trouble with the government.

Gorbachev's goals

When Gorbachev came to power, he set himself some overwhelming goals. He desperately wanted to save the Soviet Union from economic collapse and make life better for the Soviet people. He also sought to maintain the Soviet Union's position as a world superpower, realizing that if the economy failed, his country would lose

that status. Gorbachev also wanted to democratize the government, that is, to give people a voice. He hoped this would give them a stake in the new system so that they would be willing to back his reforms and help him rebuild the economy. As he put it on one occasion, "A house can be put in order only by a person who feels that he owns the house."

Gorbachev was up against a major obstacle in trying to reform the Soviet Union—the Communist party. Gorbachev knew that to achieve his goals he had to shift power away from the party. For in the Soviet Union, the party controlled everything, including the economy and the government. Some party members favored reform, but most fiercely resisted his ideas. Even though he did not want to challenge the party's position overall, Gorbachev wanted to move away from the total rule of the Communist party. He thought he could remain a loyal Communist and yet persuade the party to give up some of its power. He hoped its members would see that it was better to give up some power than have the country collapse and lose it all. Gorbachev had no intention of setting up a capitalist democracy like the United States. He believed in socialism but felt his country would benefit from the introduction of some democratic and capitalist practices. Gorbachev meant to save both the country *and* the party and, toward this end, offered a concrete plan of action.

Glasnost

The first part, and the foundation, of Gorbachev's reform plan was glasnost, which means speaking out, or openness. Under this policy, Gorbachev hoped to achieve true freedom of expression in the Soviet Union. He thought that if the people really knew how desperate the situation was in the Soviet Union—and if they were given the right to speak openly—they would support him in his search to find answers. In this way, he hoped to defeat the opponents of reform. Without glasnost, Gorbachev's other reforms would not have been possible.

Under glasnost, Gorbachev took steps to lift censorship. After decades of silence, it seemed as if a dam had broken. A flood of books, newspaper articles, films, and television programs appeared criticizing, rather than glorifying, the Soviet system and its leaders. In 1989, for example, the *Moscow News* ran a story about the 1986 explosion at the Chernobyl nuclear power plant in Ukraine. The story criticized the fact that Gorbachev's government, in spite of glasnost, had at first tried to cover up the disaster. The story's headline was: "The Big Lie." Few newspapers would have dared to criticize the government so openly before Gorbachev's reforms.

Gorbachev also eased measures against dissidents. Among others, he freed Andrei Sakharov, the famous physicist and the inventor of the Soviet Union's hydrogen bomb. Once a loyal Communist, Sakharov had grown disillusioned with the Soviet system and had become one of its chief critics. For this, Brezhnev had exiled him from Moscow without a trial.

Another part of glasnost was a greater tolerance for religion. Gorbachev made it possible for the Soviet people to once again worship as they pleased. He opened churches, temples, and mosques and allowed Bibles and other religious works to be printed again. And in 1990, the legislature ended the official Communist policy of atheism.

Restructuring the economy

Building on the foundation of glasnost, Gorbachev started restructuring different parts of So-

Andrei Sakharov, a dissident exiled from Moscow by Brezhnev, was freed under Gorbachev's new policy of glasnost.

viet society. In Russian, the word for restructuring is perestroika, so this was what his overall plan was called. It had two parts—political perestroika and economic perestroika. Gorbachev turned his attention to the economy first. In one of his speeches to the Communist party, Gorbachev described his plan:

> It is obvious that all of us must restructure ourselves—all of us . . . from worker to minister to secretary of the Party Central Committee, to leaders of the government. . . . Overall this will require immense mobilization of creative forces and the ability to . . . conduct the country's business in a new way.

As Gorbachev saw it, one of the major problems with the economy was that it was too highly centralized. The Communist party controlled everything from Moscow. Government officials working in the country's capital decided everything, including what products to produce, what prices and wages would be, how much time would be allowed for production, and how to use the country's natural resources. One result of this central planning was that growers and manufacturers could not respond accurately to local needs. For example, millions of shoes sat on store shelves because the sizes did not match the Soviet people's feet. To correct this and other problems brought about by central planning, Gorbachev began to decentralize the economy. He gave local farm and factory managers some of the power to make daily economic decisions. He felt that they had a clearer idea of what made sense for their particular business.

Members of the Russian Orthodox church carry religious images along Red Square. Under glasnost, the legislature ended the official Communist policy of atheism, making public religious processions legal.

Learning to stand on their own

Gorbachev then began to transfer businesses from government to private ownership, a process known as privatization. He allowed individuals or

Gorbachev's policy of privatization gave this family an opportunity that Soviet citizens had not experienced before—to own a share of the collective farm on which they work and share in the profits.

families to form cooperatives in small manufacturing or farming enterprises. In a cooperative, the workers own and operate the business and share the profits. Although he was still unwilling to allow farmers to own land privately, Gorbachev proposed that they lease land from the government. Under Gorbachev, private cooperatives were set up in twenty-nine kinds of businesses, including restaurants, beauty salons, banks, and advertising agencies. Before long, the Soviets had 193,000 cooperatives conducting business in their country.

Gleb Orlikhovsky, who is the business manager for a cooperative film company, described what kind of impact these new cooperatives had:

> Working for a cooperative makes people independent, free. They feel they can stand on their own. This changes their lives. They quit the Party. They think, "What do I need this swamp for?" And that's not what the system wants. The whole system is built on dependence—not independence. It's built on people's dependence on government agencies. That's what the bureaucrats don't want to see change. If it changes, then the bureaucrats and the Party lose power.

With privatization under way, Gorbachev set out to improve worker productivity by introducing incentives, or rewards. In the past, the Communist state gave its workers little reason to work hard; how much people made had nothing to do with how well they performed. They did not face the threat of being fired or receive any rewards for good work. One young Soviet television producer, Dima Mamedov, complained:

> Even if I don't work hard at it, for my job they pay me 170 rubles [about 285 dollars] a month. If the show is no good—boring—they pay me 170 rubles. If I work hard and kill myself and the show is very popular, they still pay me the same measly 170 rubles. Does that make sense?

So, workers, though secure, drifted along caring little—cogs in the great Soviet machine. Gorbachev, however, set a new standard by tying wages to performance. Workers were told they would receive more money if they produced more or if the quality of their work improved. They also faced the loss of their jobs if they did not perform well.

Gorbachev not only had to inspire Soviet laborers to work harder, but he also had to modernize Soviet factories and farms so that they could produce more. He needed money, as well as new technology, to improve outdated Soviet methods and machinery. Gorbachev opened the country to foreign investors. Some, including Pepsi-Cola and McDonald's, started businesses of their own on Soviet soil. Others formed joint ventures with Soviet interests. In these joint ventures, both parties shared the risk and split the profits. Gor-

Moscow's first McDonald's opened in 1990. A number of foreign investors, including Pepsi-Cola and McDonald's, took advantage of the new openness and set up successful businesses in the Soviet Union.

bachev went to the West for technology as well as money, buying everything from milking machines to computers.

Rebuilding the government

With economic perestroika under way, Gorbachev turned his attention to political perestroika, or rebuilding the government. Like the economy, the government was controlled by the Communist party from Moscow. To break this control and give power to the people, Gorbachev created a new legislative structure. First, he set up a lower house called the Congress of People's Deputies. Although 750 of its 2,250 members would be chosen by such organizations as the Communist party, the rest would be elected by the people. This congress met once or twice a year, and its main purpose was to select 500 of its members to sit in the upper house called the Supreme Soviet. The Supreme Soviet, though it had the same name as the old legislature, was much more independent. Its members created and passed the laws as they saw fit, no longer voting

In a move that took away some of the power from the Communist party, Gorbachev created a legislative body in which most members are elected by the people. The first session of the Congress of People's Deputies was in 1989.

the way the party dictated. Once the new legislative structure had been set up, Gorbachev scheduled elections, which were held in March 1989. These were the first elections in seventy years in which the Soviet people had a real choice. Ninety percent of them turned out to vote. Although most of those elected were Communists, some hard-line candidates were defeated and replaced by reformers. To give the people even more choice in their government, Gorbachev soon introduced another reform—the multiparty system—allowing other political parties to operate in the Soviet Union.

The end of the cold war

The changes made by Gorbachev had far-reaching effects, not just for his own citizens, but for people around the world. The Soviet leader's foreign-policy decisions were as stunning as his glasnost and perestroika. They led, among other things, to the end of the cold war between the Soviet Union and the United States. Gorbachev knew that the arms race had drained the Soviet Union of badly needed money and expertise. Only peace between the superpowers would allow him to focus all his attention on reforming his country. So, in December 1988, Gorbachev made the United States—and the world at large—an astounding offer. He announced that the Soviets would end nuclear tests, remove their missiles from Eastern Europe, and dramatically cut military spending. Gorbachev also promised to pull Soviet troops out of Eastern Europe and other places around the globe.

Gorbachev's offer surprised world leaders, who never expected the Soviet superpower to back down from its cold war stance. American president Ronald Reagan, spotting the opportunity of a lifetime, agreed to scale down American

Gorbachev (left) and President Ronald Reagan exchange copies of an arms-control treaty, agreeing to scale down each country's military power.

After fifty years of division, East and West Germany were reunited. A demonstrator pounds away at the Berlin Wall, the symbol of Soviet might.

military power. East-West tensions eased, and the cold war gradually came to an end.

The freeing of Eastern Europe

In addition to ending the hostility with the United States, Gorbachev allowed the satellite nations of Eastern Europe to break free from Soviet control. In the late 1980s, staggering economic and environmental problems caused unrest to mount among Eastern Europeans, who had long been hostile to Communist rule. Encouraged by Gorbachev's reforms, Eastern Europeans revolted against their Communist governments. One by one, with no attempt by Gorbachev to help put down the revolts, governments in Hungary, Czechoslovakia, Poland, Romania, Bulgaria, and East Germany fell.

With the fall of the East German government came the dismantling of the Berlin Wall in November 1989. This wall had become a symbol of Soviet might and of the division of the world into hostile, opposing camps. When the East German government fell, thousands of people from both sides lined the fifteen-foot-high wall. Families, separated for decades, strained to catch a glimpse of relatives through the massive crowds. All of a sudden, the Brandenburg Gate at the Berlin Wall was opened, and East Germans streamed through to West Berlin. Before long, people climbed up on top of the wall. Music filled the air from radios and guitars as people danced and sang on top of it. Armed with hammers, chisels, and sometimes just their bare hands, the German people, about to be united again after fifty years, attacked the wall and symbolically brought the Iron Curtain down with it.

Gorbachev did not send in the Red Army to prevent the collapse of the governments in East Germany or the rest of Eastern Europe. He knew the Soviet Union could not afford to funnel any more money there. He also hoped the West would help fund Soviet rebuilding and knew Western leaders would be more likely to provide aid if he stayed out of Eastern Europe. He therefore let the satellites go and protected the new relationship with the United States and other Western democracies. In the end, Gorbachev did not see his vision for his country come true. The 1989 revolution in Eastern Europe not only brought an end to the Communist bloc, but marked the beginning of the breakup of the Soviet Union.

4

The Curtain Falls

THE LOSS OF Eastern Europe was only the beginning. Before long, the curtain fell on the Soviet Union, too. Gorbachev had wanted to save both the Soviet Union and the Communist party. But the Second Russian Revolution that he had begun in 1985 swept beyond his control. Perestroika and glasnost unleashed two powerful forces: one was the people's demand for democracy, and the other was the desire of the different ethnic groups within the Soviet Union for self-rule. In the end, these forces defeated Gorbachev's purpose. They shattered the Soviet state and the center of world communism, shaking the globe to its foundations and changing history for all time.

Gorbachev loses support at home

Although Gorbachev was well liked in the West and in Eastern Europe, after a while he began to lose support at home. Before glasnost, few had dared to criticize Communist leaders, but now people could speak their minds. Before long, the ranks of Gorbachev's critics grew. The conservatives thought Gorbachev had gone too far with his reforms and wanted him to slow down. Among them were the hard-line Communists, leaders in the Red Army and the KGB (secret police), and many Moscow bureaucrats. They were the pillars

(Opposite page) Anti-government protesters raise signs in support of Russian president Boris Yeltsin and calling for the resignation of Gorbachev. Ironically, it was Gorbachev's policy of glasnost that gave people the freedom to speak out openly against the government.

of the old system and stood to lose power and influence as Gorbachev's reforms took hold.

On the other side were the democrats who wanted Gorbachev to go faster with the reforms. They included intellectuals, members of the liberal press, writers, artists, and some party members who believed that the old system should be completely destroyed. Leading this group was Russian president Boris Yeltsin, who had been dismissed from his party positions by Gorbachev for criticizing the slow pace of perestroika. Yeltsin, for example, suggested a plan that would change the Soviet Union's communist economy into a capitalist economy in five hundred days. One feature of Yeltsin's plan called for returning *all* property to private ownership, while Gorbachev had been unwilling to privatize land.

Searching for a middle ground

Gorbachev tried to stay on the middle ground between the conservatives and the democrats. He knew that to save the country, he had to destroy the totalitarian state that Stalin had built. Gorbachev, however, had no intention of doing away with communism. He planned to reform it by making it more democratic. He hoped this would help him create a better Soviet Union. In 1990, *Time* magazine asked Gorbachev what it meant to be a Communist. He replied:

> To be a communist . . . means not to be afraid of what is new, to reject obedience to any dogma, to think independently . . . to help working people realize their hopes . . . and live up to their abilities. I believe that to be a communist today means first of all to be consistently democratic and to put universal human values above everything else. . . . The Stalinist model of socialism should not be confused with true socialist theory. As we dismantle the Stalinist system, we are not retreating from socialism, but are moving toward it.

Gorbachev's unwillingness to let go of communism may have been his greatest flaw. It pleased hard-liners but cost him the support of many average Soviet citizens who no longer had any use for it. Communism had brought them continuing shortages of food, fuel, and consumer goods. Gorbachev's reforms had not improved this situation much. In some cases, daily life for the average Soviet citizen had become even harder. Among other things, unemployment, once unheard of in the Soviet Union, now threatened millions of workers. As the Soviet Union scaled back its military, for example, about five million defense-industry workers stood to lose their jobs.

The republics revolt

Not only had the people grown weary of communism, but many of them—especially the non-Russian citizens of the U.S.S.R.—were tired of being included in the Soviet Union itself. Throughout Gorbachev's time in power, unrest had been growing in the country's non-Russian republics. Citizens in these republics, many of whom had retained their own cultures, wanted more say in their own political and economic affairs. When Gorbachev gave the Soviet people greater freedoms and released Eastern Europe from the Soviet grasp, the seething discontent among the non-Russian peoples burst out into the open. The strength of their desire for freedom caught Gorbachev by surprise. He had underestimated the powerful feelings of nationalism within the Soviet Union. His insistence on keeping the Soviet state intact only sharpened the conflict with the restless republics.

Cries for self-rule echoed loudest in the Baltic states (on Russia's western border). During World War II, Stalin had brutally absorbed the three Baltic countries—Estonia, Latvia, and Lithua-

A sign at a gas station in Moscow reads "No Petrol." Gorbachev's efforts did little to improve daily life in the Soviet Union, where shortages of fuel, food, and consumer goods continued.

Lithuanians demonstrate in 1991 in support of their republic's independence.

nia—into the Soviet Union. Baltic residents had never accepted Soviet domination, however, and saw the new era in Soviet leadership and reform as an opportunity for gaining independence. In August 1989, demonstrating their desire for freedom, more than one million people joined hands and formed a human "freedom chain" extending nearly four hundred miles from Estonia through Latvia to Lithuania.

A final crackdown in Lithuania

Of all the Baltic countries, Lithuania was the most determined to obtain its freedom. In March 1990, Lithuanians went to the polls to vote in the country's first multiparty elections. Lithuanian nationalists defeated many Communists to win a majority of seats in the legislature. Inspired by this victory, Lithuania declared its independence.

But Lithuania had misjudged just how far Gorbachev was willing to go. He had freed Eastern Europe, but he was not about to do the same for the Baltics or other Soviet republics. Gorbachev feared that if he let Lithuania go it would start a chain reaction that would tear the Soviet Union apart. To force Lithuania back into line, Gorbachev cracked down. In a show of Soviet might, he cut off all supplies of oil and gas and sent tanks rumbling through the streets of Vilnius, the Lithuanian capital. At first, Gorbachev avoided using outright force to bring Lithuania in line. But eventually he sent in troops with orders to do whatever was needed to get the situation under control. Unarmed Lithuanians threw up barriers around their government buildings, trying to defend themselves against Soviet tanks and troops with their bare hands. But the Soviets broke through the barriers and seized some of the buildings, killing fifteen civilians.

Commenting on this tragedy, Lithuanian president Vytautus Landsbergis said, "The spirit of Stalin is walking the Kremlin again." The Soviet people, feeling exactly the same way, saw the Lithuanian tragedy as Gorbachev's darkest hour. There was a tremendous outcry against him for the actions he had taken there. At the same time,

Armed Soviet soldiers keep an eye on demonstrating Lithuanian nationalists. Fifteen unarmed civilians were killed when soldiers broke through the human barriers and seized the government buildings.

A committee of the Congress of the People's Deputies, chaired by Gorbachev, meets to draft the Union Treaty. This treaty gave the republics the power to secede from the Soviet Union.

Lithuania had withstood Gorbachev's anger, and in so doing served as a powerful inspiration to the other republics.

The Union Treaty

With the republics in revolt, Gorbachev made a final attempt to save the Soviet Union. He drew up a new treaty giving all of the republics some sovereignty, or self-rule, and setting up a loose union of states. This Union Treaty, as it was called, gave many of the central government's powers to the republics. It gave them the right to make their own decisions about their economy and local politics. The treaty also gave the republics the power to secede, or withdraw, from the Soviet Union, which would be renamed the Union of *Sovereign* Socialist Republics. Because the Soviet system had made the republics dependent on one another, Gorbachev truly believed they would have trouble standing alone. For this reason, he hoped to keep as many of the republics together as possible. In the end, all the republics except the three Baltic states and Armenia, Moldova, and Georgia—which wanted complete independence—agreed to join the new union. The

Union Treaty was scheduled to be signed on August 20, 1991.

The August coup

On Sunday, August 18, 1991, a little before 5:00 P.M., two black limousines rolled quietly up to the gate of Gorbachev's vacation home in the Crimea. Inside the cars were some of the conspirators who had come to inform him that they had staged a coup d'etat, or sudden revolt, and that he had been ousted. Furious, Gorbachev replied, "Only suicidal killers could propose to . . . reintroduce a totalitarian regime in the country now." They placed him under house arrest and, leaving him heavily guarded, returned to Moscow. Remembering what had happened to Nicholas II and his family decades earlier, the Gorbachevs feared for their lives. Nevertheless, the family promised to stand together, saying they were "ready to share everything . . . to the end."

Eight of Gorbachev's closest associates planned and carried out the coup. They included, among others, the vice president, the prime minister, the defense minister, the chief of the KGB, and Gorbachev's personal aide. They planned to drop the Union Treaty, return to the absolute rule of the Communist party, and force the republics back into line. The conspirators outlawed all other political parties and closed down all opposition newspapers and television stations. They put the military on alert and ordered troops and tanks to Moscow. It was later discovered that these men had even ordered 250,000 pairs of handcuffs, which showed that they were prepared to use force against the people.

The people fight back

The coup organizers failed to understand the changes that had taken place in the Soviet Union.

They had misjudged how deeply opposed the people were to the old Soviet system. Rallied by Russian president Boris Yeltsin, tens of thousands of citizens vowed to stop the conspirators and save the freedoms that had at long last come to their country. Though Gorbachev had lost a good deal of support, the people did not want to return to the old ways. Glasnost and perestroika had changed the nation.

It was almost noon on August 19—Day Two of the coup—when columns of armored tanks rolled into Moscow on orders from coup leaders. The tanks surrounded the Russian Parliament Building, also called the White House. Not knowing how the soldiers inside the tanks would react, Yeltsin climbed on top of one tank. Speaking passionately to the crowd, he condemned the coup and called for the people's help:

> Citizens of Russia . . . the legally elected president of the country was removed from power. . . . We

Yeltsin, atop an armored tank, urges the Soviet people to resist the hard-line takeover of the central government in Moscow.

are dealing with a rightist, reactionary, anticonstitutional coup. . . . Accordingly, we proclaim all decisions of this committee to be unlawful. . . . We appeal to the citizens of Russia to give fitting rebuff to the putschists [conspirators who plot to overthrow a government] and demand a return of the country to normal constitutional development.

Responding to Yeltsin's passionate plea, Soviet soldiers turned their tanks away from the White House and pledged to defend the Russian president.

Shortly after Yeltsin's speech, the soldiers turned their tanks away from the White House, and pledged to defend the Russian president. People from all over the city streamed to the White House, chanting Yeltsin's name.

Everyone believed the coup plotters would stage an attack on Yeltsin at the White House on August 20. To prepare, Moscow residents, following the Lithuanians' example, built barricades with city buses, park benches, and sewer pipes. Unarmed, they stood fast at these barricades ready to face down the expected attack by additional Soviet tanks and troops. Yeltsin's guardians stayed outside the White House all night to make sure nothing happened to him. And Yeltsin, who had been urged to flee, remained with those who were ready to die to protect him. "I'm not going anywhere. I'd rather die here, with you, in a fight to the death," declared Yeltsin. But the attack never came. Officers refused to carry out the conspirators' orders. Soldiers, faced with signs that read "Soldiers, Don't Shoot Your Mothers," would not open fire. Before long, the soldiers had joined the people in the streets. Protesters decorated the tanks with flowers and Russian flags. Members of the KGB also mutinied and joined the throngs. One man was asked if he had come to the White House to save his country. He replied:

> No. I am here for myself. I am like everybody else in this sorry excuse for a country. I went to school, graduated . . . got a job. . . . And I hated every minute of what I did. You know why? Because I saw that nobody . . . was interested in anything except beating drums about fulfilling the plan. We never fulfilled it, mind you. We played around with the stats, we lied, we stuck a pillow here, padded a little there. . . . We laughed at how we were fooling the government, and we stole from ourselves. We lived in a world that stood on its head and thought that was the only way to live.

> Then, along came Gorbachev—and everything changed. I founded a co-op. I started doing work that I loved. . . . I started making real money instead of pretending to work for pretended pay. . . . I got married and had a son—and I want him to be proud of his father. . . . That is what I am here for. For myself, for my son, for the right to be what I can be. I will die for that, trust me.

The political climate changes

By Thursday, August 22, the coup had collapsed, and Gorbachev was back in the Kremlin. Upon his return to Moscow, he stated that he once again had "full control of the situation." But the political climate had changed, and Gorbachev was mistaken. The tanks and troops were gone, and the square in front of the White House had been cleared. But Gorbachev's time as leader of the Soviet Union had come to an end. A new leader had emerged—Boris Yeltsin. As Russia's first-elected president, Yeltsin was already in control of the most powerful Soviet republic. During the coup, he had run not only the Russian republic, but the whole Soviet Union. Now, he had the power, and Gorbachev was no more than a figurehead. Yeltsin and the Soviet people had rebelled to save Gorbachev's reforms, but not to save Gorbachev himself.

The collapse of the coup meant the end of the Communist party, because the party had been behind it, staging its last grab for power. The at-

© 1991 by NEA, Inc. 4A

ON THE ROPES

tempted coup demonstrated the party's unwillingness to go along with reform and its desire for totalitarian rule. Hundreds and hundreds of people gathering in the streets to celebrate the downfall of the coup shouted, "Down with the Communist party!" One man said, "We are all sick of the Communists. They have been strangling us for seventy years." Believing that the time had come to finish off Soviet communism, Yeltsin closed the main Communist party newspaper, *Pravda*, and forced Gorbachev to agree to halt all party activities in the Russian Republic. Gorbachev tried to defend the party even though he knew it was behind the coup. He still believed that it could be saved if some changes were made. But within a few days, Gorbachev changed his mind. He stepped down as the party's general secretary and banned it from taking part in government, the

Workers in Riga, Latvia, dismantle a huge statue of Lenin just days after the coup's collapse. The toppling of monuments such as this symbolized the fall of the Communist party and the coming end of the Soviet Union.

military, and the KGB. He padlocked party headquarters and seized the party's property, including cars, publishing houses, printing plants, and office buildings.

All over the Soviet Union, people took this as a sign that the Communist party was officially dead. They toppled huge statues of Lenin and other well-known Communists. The Soviet people even took Lenin's embalmed body out of Moscow's Red Square tomb, where for years it had been on display for millions of loyal Communists, and buried it in a regular cemetery.

The Soviet Union is shattered

The collapse of the coup shattered the Soviet Union itself, not just the Communist party. The party, the KGB, and the Red Army had been the pillars holding up the Soviet state. Now, these pillars had crumbled, and there was nothing to hold up the state anymore. When Gorbachev met with the leaders of the republics, he found that they would no longer take orders from him. One by one, the republics officially declared their independence. The Baltics moved first, taking advantage of the chaos in the Soviet government to grab for *real* independence. Then, Ukraine broke free. Because it was a vital agricultural and industrial area, losing Ukraine was devastating to the Soviet Union. Ukraine's departure set off a chain reaction among the rest of the republics. Soon, Belarus, Moldova, Azerbaijan, Kyrgyzstan, Uzbekistan, Tajikistan, Georgia, Armenia, and Russia had declared their freedom. Armenian president Levon Ter-Petrosian expressed the views of many republic leaders when he said, "The whole of the central government has completely outlived itself. It is dead. It has committed suicide."

5

The Death of a Dream

THE FALL OF the Soviet Union was for some the death of a dream. Communism had promised a bright future, but it had failed. And now the dream was gone. Left in its place was reality, which amounted to a host of problems. Until glasnost, the Soviet Union had tried to keep its troubles hidden from the outside world and even from its own citizens. But once the Communist party and the Soviet state were gone, the curtain lifted to reveal the true condition of the nation— or really fifteen nations. Economies everywhere were ruined. The environment was a disaster. The health of the people was at risk. Ethnic hatreds threatened to tear apart the former Soviet republics. The Soviet Union's survival was no longer an issue. But the survival of its former citizens, trying to build new lives amid all these problems, became the number one concern.

(Opposite page) Neither communism nor perestroika succeeded in improving living conditions for most Soviet citizens. In one Russian mining region, as in other parts of the former Soviet Union, prospects for a better life seem dim. This woman and her two children live in a house without central heat, water, or flushing toilets.

Economic decline

Between Gorbachev's first days in office and the Soviet Union's collapse, the economy and the people's standard of living had declined. Soviet citizens had never lived very well, but under the Communist system they had at least been able to

65

The Former Soviet Republics

MOLDOVA
LATVIA
ESTONIA
LITHUANIA
BELARUS
UKRAINE
AZERBAIJAN
GEORGIA
UZBEKISTAN
KAZAKHSTAN
ARMENIA
TURKMENISTAN
KYRGYZSTAN
TAJIKISTAN
RUSSIA

fulfill their basic needs. Under perestroika, which was supposed to improve daily life, people struggled just to survive. Although wages were higher than they had been before Gorbachev's reforms, the average monthly salary—about 3,000 rubles, or 9 dollars—did not go very far. This amount had to pay for housing, utilities, medical care, and education—all of which had been provided at little or no cost under the Communist system.

Costs for rent, fuel, and especially food, rose rapidly. The price of electricity, oil, and gas jumped so high that many people went without heat and hot water. Households in some areas had hot water for only a few hours each morning; family members made all three meals, washed the dishes and clothes, bathed, and set aside drinking water before they went to work or school.

The most serious concern for many families, however, was finding enough food to eat, given low wages and skyrocketing prices. A pound of sausage or butter, for example, cost an entire month's wages. Most ordinary citizens spent the bulk of their income on food, and they often ate only one meal a day. Many people lived on bread and water alone. One of the reasons for such high prices was that food was scarce, and this was partly because of Gorbachev's perestroika. Although perestroika was a restructuring of the Soviet economy, Gorbachev was still trying to control the economy from Moscow. He expected state and collective farms to deliver their targeted crops to the central government, which would then distribute the food throughout the nation. Instead, the farmers hoarded food to get higher prices in the new private markets or on the black market—an illegal market where a wide variety of goods can be bought for generally very high

A woman peers into a display case in a Moscow food store, only to find there is no food to buy. Extreme shortages of food continue to plague the former Soviet Union.

prices. The black market had always existed, but it expanded dramatically during perestroika.

Once housing, fuel, and food were paid for, there was generally no money left for increasingly expensive consumer goods. Most people had old televisions, washing machines, and refrigerators. If they broke, families usually did not have enough money to fix them—let alone replace them. Clothing became a luxury. Family members shared each other's clothes and rarely bought anything new.

Increasing unemployment added to the problems. In the first year after the fall of the Soviet Union, unemployment rose from 100,000 to 1,000,000. This was hard for people to accept in a country where the old government had guaranteed every worker a job. The state had run all the farms and factories, and when it began to step out and cut off support to inefficient state enterprises, thousands were thrown out of work. Thousands more lost their jobs as the defense industry was cut back with the end of the cold war. And the new cooperatives and other private businesses just getting started could not yet take up the slack. Some of the jobless have even taken their own lives. At one steel plant, a worker said, "It's quite common to commit suicide by throwing oneself into the liquid ore."

A nightmarish legacy

The dismal economy was not the only problem revealed when the Soviet Union fell. Environmental pollution was so great in some parts of the former Soviet Union that nothing will ever live in these areas again. This pollution came from a variety of sources. Factories had no pollution controls. Their smokestacks pumped unfiltered smoke into the air. Because of this, thousands of miles of forests were harmed, and crop yields

fell. Waste was dumped into rivers and lakes that were used for drinking water. This included liquid waste from factories and farms, untreated sewage, and radioactive waste from nuclear plants producing weapons and energy. The contaminated rivers flowed into the seas, spreading pollution to other countries.

A lack of pollution controls allowed factories to pump unfiltered smoke into the air, destroying forests and creating serious environmental problems.

These problems did not suddenly occur under Gorbachev. They had been building for decades and were kept secret by Soviet leaders. In the drive to turn the Soviet Union into a modern, industrial power, the country's government had ignored the destruction taking place in the environment.

The legacy of environmental destruction can be seen most vividly in the health of the people. A group of high school students from Brateyevo, an industrial area on the outskirts of Moscow, described the effects of pollution on the local residents:

> We exist here but you can't call it living in the
> normal sense. Grass doesn't grow in this area.
> Trees are dying. Gas exhaust from the oil refinery

The 1986 explosion of the Chernobyl nuclear reactor spewed radiation across parts of the Soviet Union and into Europe. About ten thousand people have died from Chernobyl's nuclear fallout.

causes headaches, dizziness, loss of attention. It is hard to exercise here. Many gasp for air even after light exercise. We have no place for leisure.

Nuclear pollution has left the most damaging health legacy. The gravest example of this was the destruction caused by the 1986 explosion of the Chernobyl nuclear reactor in Ukraine. The reactor used atomic power to create energy, which was then converted into electricity for people in the surrounding area. On April 25, the operators at the reactor made several mistakes. Although they tried to correct them, the reactor finally exploded. The blast, which shot flames 1,500 feet high, was 300 to 400 times more powerful than the atomic bomb the United States dropped on Hiroshima, Japan, during World War II. Within a matter of hours, people in the area began to show signs of radiation sickness. Not only the people, but the land, the crops, and the animals were poisoned. Carried by the wind, the huge cloud of radiation created by the blast moved through parts of the Soviet Union and across Europe. After Chernobyl, stomach and kidney illnesses in Ukrainians increased by 450 percent. People in nearby Belarus received even more of the fallout, or poisonous radioactive dust. They had more cases of thyroid cancer and leukemia. Officials believe that four million people have been affected. About ten thousand have already died from Chernobyl's nuclear fallout.

Bloody battlegrounds

Just as environment and health problems have come to light since the Soviet Union's collapse, so have tensions between different ethnic groups. Ethnic hatreds have existed for a long time, but they surfaced only rarely while the Soviet system maintained tight control. When Gorbachev's glas-

A woman mourns the destruction of her house in Moldova, where long-suppressed ethnic hatreds have exploded into violence.

nost gave people freedom to speak out, tensions between ethnic groups started to build. Then, when the Soviet system collapsed, long-suppressed hatreds exploded in waves of violence. Ethnic warfare has claimed thousands of lives all across the former Soviet Union. One conflict area is in the tiny country of Moldova, which Stalin seized from Romania during World War II. Ethnic Romanians, who make up the majority of the population, seek to undo Stalin's work by reuniting their country with Romania. Ethnic Russians and Ukrainians who live there do not want to become part of Romania. They want to separate from Moldova and form a new state. Violence in Moldova is even more worrisome because it could spill over into heavily populated Ukraine. There is also war in Georgia as South Ossetians and Abkhazians battle to break away. And there are many clashes between Muslim groups, like the Uzbeks and the Meshkhetian Turks, in the Fergana Valley of Central Asia.

A blood feud

One of the bloodiest ethnic conflicts of all has been between Armenia and Azerbaijan over an area called Nagorno-Karabakh. This independent area lies within Muslim Azerbaijan but is mostly populated with Christian Armenians. That is because it once belonged to Armenia, but Stalin awarded it to Azerbaijan. The Armenians believe that Nagorno-Karabakh should be a part of their country because most of the people there are Armenians who want to rejoin their homeland. The Armenians also want to be apart from the Azerbaijanis because the Azerbaijanis are related to the Ottoman Turks, who massacred almost a million Armenians in 1915. The Azerbaijanis do not want to lose any of their land, which is a symbol of their nation. They feel the Soviet Union

A woman mourns the deaths of her husband and son, both killed in the ethnic conflicts tearing apart Azerbaijan and Armenia. She holds an enlarged copy of her son's Communist party membership card.

stripped them of everything else, including their valuable oil. They also see the Armenians as rich neighbors who were favored by the Soviet Union. Azerbaijanis want all of the Armenians in Nagorno-Karabakh to leave so that only Azerbaijanis live in their homeland.

Under Gorbachev, the Armenians thought they had a chance of getting Nagorno-Karabakh back. In the cities, as many as 500,000 people marched, carrying banners that said "Karabakh Is Part of Armenia!" and "Karabakh Is a Test Case for Perestroika!" The Azerbaijanis feared that the Armenians might be successful, so they warned Gorbachev that giving this area to the Armenians would anger the Soviet Union's fifty million Muslims. Gorbachev was also afraid that if he changed one border, he would have to change others. Caught between his reforms and his desire to preserve the Soviet state, Gorbachev put the area under Moscow's rule. But this did not solve anything, and the two republics went to war in 1988.

Terrible massacres have taken place on both sides. So far, more than five thousand people have died in this war. In Sumgait, Azerbaijan, mobs hunted out Armenians and killed them. Asya Arakelyan described what happened to her:

> The Azerbaijanis came all dressed in black. They went through every building . . . shouting . . .

Demonstrators in Moscow protest the massacre of Armenians in Sumgait, Azerbaijan. One banner demands "Full openness in the Sumgait trial," another pleads "Acknowledge the genocide of Armenians in Sumgait."

"Death to Armenians.". . . They threw me down . . . and started wildly beating me with anything they could lay their hands on. And those axes and knives—it was terrible. . . . Then they dumped some gasoline over my body and burned me. I didn't know that right next to me, they had gone at my husband. They hacked him with an ax and burned his body.

Azerbaijanis, too, fled from violence that was turned on them by Armenians. One Azerbaijani family, the Guliyevs, were getting ready to move to Baku, Azerbaijan. Before they could leave, their son Magaran was murdered at the railroad station by Armenians who attacked him with hammers, axes, and screwdrivers. When his mother went to get his body, an Armenian soldier said, "Why are you crying? Is this not enough for you? We should have annihilated all of your kind, as we did this one."

Lenin's dream of a new Soviet citizen, who would rise above ethnic boundaries to serve the Soviet state, was just that—a dream. If it had not been for the Communist party, the Red Army, and the KGB, these bitter rivalries probably would have surfaced many years earlier. And as a result of being suppressed for so long, these rivalries often exploded with greater violence when they finally did surface. The Soviet Union left a legacy of ethnic hatred, along with economic and health-related disasters. And it was up to the countries forming in its wake to try to find a way to solve these problems.

6

Building Up from the Ruins

ON DECEMBER 25, 1991, Mikhail Gorbachev stepped down as president of the Soviet Union. At the Kremlin, the red Soviet flag, with its gold hammer and sickle, was lowered for the last time. With the Soviet Union and its all-powerful Communist party in ruins, the newly independent post-Soviet states had to rebuild their economic and political systems. Most wanted to set up capitalist economies and democratic governments. This would prove to be very difficult because the Soviet people had no experience with either. Many of the new states decided their best chance for success was to work together, but there was always conflict brewing between them. More and more, each state began to go its own way. The future remains uncertain. No one really knows what will rise from the ashes of the once mighty giant that was the Soviet Union.

(Opposite page) The newly raised Russian flag flutters in the wind over the Kremlin. It has replaced the Soviet flag, which was removed immediately following Gorbachev's resignation.

Setting up the Commonwealth

By the time Gorbachev had stepped down as president of the Soviet Union, eleven of the fifteen republics had already formed a loose-knit union of governments called the Commonwealth of Independent States (CIS). Within the Com-

Leaders of eleven former Soviet republics, which make up the Commonwealth of Independent States, meet to discuss foreign affairs and economic and defense policies.

monwealth, each country would retain control over its own affairs but would work with the other member states to coordinate policy in such areas of shared interest as economics, foreign affairs, and defense. CIS members included Russia, Ukraine, Belarus, Moldova, Armenia, Azerbaijan, Kazakhstan, Turkmenistan, Uzbekistan, Tajikistan, and Kyrgyzstan. Only the three Baltic countries—Latvia, Lithuania, and Estonia—and Georgia refused to take part. They felt joining the CIS would jeopardize their newfound independence. Despite the absence of these four countries, Commonwealth leaders moved forward and met in January 1992. Hope filled the air. But mounting conflicts among the member states soon sorely tested the Commonwealth and jeopardized its future.

Russia dominates the Commonwealth

One of the main areas of disagreement had to do with Russia's place in the CIS. All of the countries in the CIS were supposed to be equal, but the other states felt Russia was dominating Commonwealth affairs. As the largest and richest Soviet republic, Russia had always had more power than the others. When the Soviet Union fell, it took over the Soviet embassy in Washington, D.C., and claimed its seat on the United Nations' Security Council. Russia viewed itself as the rightful successor to the Soviet Union and its actions gave other countries the idea that this was true. As a result, the United States and other countries often treated Russia as the leader of the Commonwealth. The other Commonwealth states were angered by this. They had just gotten rid of one dictatorial central government, and they did not want to submit to another. This issue continues to cause problems.

Dividing up the Soviet war machine

In addition to the concern over Russia's position in the CIS, the member states also argued over how to divide up the huge Soviet war machine, which consisted of almost four million soldiers and thousands of tanks, airplanes, and ships. One of the biggest disagreements developed between Russia and Ukraine over the Black Sea Fleet. With its 70,000 sailors and 350 ships, this fleet was one of the most powerful in the world. Ukraine had no ships for its new navy and laid claim to the Black Sea Fleet, which was based in southern Ukraine's Crimean Peninsula. Not wanting to relinquish power, however, Russia was determined to keep the Black Sea Fleet. Finally, in August 1992, Russia and Ukraine agreed to divide the fleet after three years of joint control. This temporarily quieted the bad feelings between the two countries but really just postponed the problem.

The former Soviet Union's huge arsenal of nuclear weapons also caused a difficult debate among CIS members. Four of the new states—Russia, Ukraine, Belarus, and Kazakhstan—possessed all of the Soviet Union's nuclear weapons. Early on, CIS leaders agreed that the Commonwealth should take control of these weapons. They selected Russia, which had inherited the Soviet Union's place as an established nuclear power, to house and supervise them. All of the Commonwealth countries would have to agree, however, before Russia could use them. Under this agreement, Belarus, Ukraine, and Kazakhstan promised to either destroy their nuclear weapons or to turn them over to Russia. This agreement was designed to prevent the emergence of any new nuclear states that could threaten global security.

After making this agreement, Ukraine and Kazakhstan became uneasy over the amount of power the new weapons would give Russia. They

Submarines, which make up some of the hundreds of vessels of the Black Sea Fleet, lie moored in a Ukrainian port. Russia and Ukraine disagreed about how to divide the huge fleet, once one of the most powerful in the world.

feared that Russia would become even more dominant over them and the other Commonwealth states with these weapons under its control. Despite these fears, Ukraine and Kazakhstan have begun to turn over their weapons to Russia.

Debates over economic affairs

Along with the dispute over nuclear weapons, debates have also arisen over economic affairs. Lack of cooperation remains the central problem for the Commonwealth. One clear example is an unwillingness among the member states to trade products freely. The Soviet Union was structured so that each republic grew or made certain products not found in the others. This system forced the republics to depend on each other. After the Soviet Union's collapse, many of the new countries refused to allow products to leave their borders even though they, too, needed products made or grown in other states. This was due to ethnic tensions and a desire to take care of their own people first. Ukraine stopped supplying food to Russian Siberia. Russia cut off oil and gas supplies to other CIS countries. And because of war in Georgia, Azerbaijan, and Armenia, many fruit shipments stopped.

Fighting over price controls

Another example of this lack of cooperation was the disagreement between Russia and Ukraine over price controls. Under Soviet communism, the government controlled prices on most goods by setting and keeping them artificially low. Under capitalism, prices are determined by supply and demand. Supply is the amount of a product that is available, and demand is the amount that people want to buy. For example, if everyone wants soccer balls, but only a few have been produced, the price of a soccer ball is likely to be high. On the other hand, if many balls have been produced, but everyone already has one, the price will be low to try to encourage people to buy.

Although Gorbachev pushed through reforms that moved the Soviet Union toward a capitalist economy based on supply and demand, he left government price controls in place for many goods. Yeltsin, who complained throughout the Gorbachev era that reforms were moving too slowly, wanted to move ahead quickly and lift these controls. When controls are lifted, prices generally rise. Yeltsin and the leaders of the other Commonwealth countries knew that higher prices in Russia would lead to higher prices in the other states. Ukraine, which still imported many different products from Russia, was especially worried about the effect of higher prices on its citizens.

Ukrainian president Leonid Kravchuk urged Yeltsin to postpone the lifting of price controls until the chaos following the Soviet Union's fall lessened and he could get Ukrainians used to the idea of higher prices. Yeltsin only agreed to a short delay and then moved ahead anyway. Knowing prices would rise because of Russia's action, Ukraine and the other CIS states then lifted price controls, too.

Quarreling over money

Russia and Ukraine fought not only over lifting price controls, but also over the money supply. The ruble was the common currency used in the Soviet Union. Early on, Commonwealth leaders agreed that they would continue to use the ruble as the common currency of the CIS. Russia, however, because of Soviet centralization, had all the presses for printing rubles. The people in Ukraine needed rubles to buy food, but Russia, steeped in chaos, had not shipped Ukraine its supply for

Vodka, a very popular drink in Russia, is one of the few consumer goods which retains government price controls.

some time. Tired of being dependent on Russia, Ukraine decided to set up its own money system. Other CIS countries may follow Ukraine's lead.

Shoppers get a taste of the free-market system in one of the many former state-owned businesses that have been sold at auction to private entrepreneurs.

Remaking Russia

As the Commonwealth wrestles with economic problems, each country is also trying to work out its own solutions. Because Russia is the largest and most powerful state in the CIS, any reforms that take place there often affect the entire Commonwealth. As leader of Russia, Yeltsin has faced a huge task. He has had to remake his country.

To jolt the sick Russian economy back to health, Yeltsin decided to use a reform plan called shock therapy. This plan calls for setting up a market economy as rapidly as possible by lifting all government price controls and privatizing all factories and farms. Although this approach has worked in other countries, it can be very painful for the people. Life tends to get worse before it gets better.

LURIE ©1992 International Copyright by CARTOONEWS Inc., N.Y.C., USA

Dinner in Russia

In January 1992, Yeltsin took the first step in shock therapy by freeing most prices from government control and allowing them to be set by supply and demand. Only such basic goods as milk, bread, medicines, vodka, and heating oil were still controlled by the government. In Russia alone, most prices rose tenfold after the controls were lifted. Yeltsin hoped that when prices went up, farmers would bring the food they had been hoarding to market and fill up the empty shelves. And this happened to a degree. But prices rose so high that most people were not able to buy many products. To offset the rise in prices, the Russian government raised wages, but this did not help much because prices had risen much higher than wages. Yuri Pronin, a Moscow resident, describes life under these reforms:

> I used to be an artist and earned quite a bit, but I became sick. Under the Communists, I could at least

survive on the 30 rubles a month I got for my disability and on money from my artwork. We didn't live well, but we lived with peace of mind. Now life is a struggle.

Privatizing Russia

After lifting government price controls, Yeltsin moved to the next step in shock therapy and began to privatize farms and factories owned by the Russian government. He knew that once these enterprises were privately owned, there would be competition between them. And he hoped it would help increase the quantity and quality of Russian food and consumer products. This, in turn, would make life easier for the Russian people who had already suffered so much.

Although Gorbachev had begun to privatize state enterprises, he had stopped short of where Yeltsin wanted to go. Yeltsin wanted *all* farms and factories in private hands, while Gorbachev, under pressure from hard-liners in the Communist party, had continued to support some dying state enterprises. And Gorbachev had never been able to bring himself to privatize land. Just after Russia passed a law allowing Russian farmers to buy land from the state, Gorbachev shared his views:

> Although in favor of the market, I do not accept private ownership of land. Do with me what you will, I do not accept it. A lease, even for one hundred years . . . and with inheritance—yes! But private ownership with the right to sell land—that I do not accept. . . . Should I renounce my grandfather, who . . . was a collective-farm chairman for seventeen years? I cannot go against my father. Should I reject whole generations? Did they live in vain?

More determined than Gorbachev to break away from the old system, Yeltsin began to cut off government financial support to Russia's huge, outdated state factories. Then, he carried the process one step further by giving each citizen a privatiza-

Workers stack millions of privatization vouchers to be distributed to 150 million people across Russia. The vouchers entitle Russians to buy land and shares of state-owned factories.

tion voucher. These vouchers were like checks and could be used to buy shares of state-owned factories, which would soon be auctioned off.

Encouraged by Yeltsin's voucher program, some Russians are moving ahead. One man bought a truck with the vouchers and started a successful dog-food business. The truck cost 190,000 rubles, or 475 dollars. His office is a ramshackle hut. But he earns five times what the average person makes. He said, "There are so many shortages and undeveloped fields here. If you want to work, you can get rich."

These privatization vouchers also entitle the Russian people to buy land. At long last, people can own their own farms. Yeltsin has already begun to break up some state and collective farms to free up land. During the first year after the fall of the Soviet Union, around eighty thousand farmers, or 4 percent of Russia's farmers, bought land and set up their own farms.

Yeltsin encouraged not only private ownership of factories and farms, but private trading. Though there were not many laws yet governing the new market system, Yeltsin declared that anyone could buy or sell anything anywhere. Now, Russia's new entrepreneurs, or organizers of businesses, stand on the street corners in Moscow and other cities, selling everything from Japanese tape recorders to Dutch chocolates. Among the street sellers are often women selling one or two items—a pair of boots or a family heirloom. They are trying to make money just to feed themselves or their families. However, along with private trading has come a tremendous growth in the black market and street crime.

A stable ruble

In addition to freeing prices and privatizing state enterprises, Yeltsin has also tried to set up a stable money system. In a stable money system, there is little inflation, which is an increase in the amount of money in circulation and a resulting rise in prices. When inflation is kept to a minimum, prices are more stable and a country's currency—in this case the ruble—has value. During 1992, inflation in Russia reached 1,000 percent a year, and the ruble dramatically dropped in value until it was almost worthless. At one point, it took 400 rubles to equal 1 dollar. Yeltsin knew he had to move fast. For in order for Russia to receive badly needed Western aid and attract Western businesses, the ruble had to have equal value with the currencies of other countries.

To try to increase the value of the ruble, Yeltsin planned to cut down on government spending. He hoped that ending government support to dying

Two Moscow street vendors sell used goods in hopes of earning money to live on.

Soviet enterprises and cutting military spending would help. If the government cut its spending, there would be less money in circulation, which meant inflation would decrease and the value of the ruble would increase. Then, the rise in prices might not be so steep, and people could buy more goods.

As time has passed, Yeltsin has found himself fighting a growing number of people who want to stop or slow down his reforms and even some who want to remove him from office. As daily life continues to deteriorate under shock therapy, some ordinary citizens, who have been Yeltsin's main supporters, have begun to desert him. Soon after he freed prices, angry consumers in cities throughout Russia rioted, staging strikes and smashing store windows. Millions of people fear that they will lose their jobs as government-

owned farms and factories close. Most see no value in Yeltsin's privatization vouchers and plan to sell theirs for money. One woman said, "What's worth investing in? Everything is going bankrupt." Another said, "I have three kids—I need the money. My factory won't take these vouchers—they're just toilet paper."

The challenge of a lifetime

This loss of support has hurt Yeltsin and made Russia more vulnerable to those who want to abandon the path of reform. Since the fall of the Soviet Union, new Communist parties have formed, and many of them long for a return to Stalinist rule. At the other extreme are the Russian nationalists, who want a return to the Russian Empire, when their country grew by seizing other people's territory. These two groups, usually so far apart, have joined together against Yeltsin. Their power base is the old Soviet legislature— the Congress of Peoples' Deputies—which was elected before the fall of communism and the Soviet Union.

As criticism mounts, even members of Yeltsin's own government have spoken out against him. He has had to go before the Russian legislature more than once to defend his reforms and himself as leader of Russia. At one meeting, the mood was so ugly that members even physically attacked one another. Although Yeltsin has been forced to partially retreat from reform, so far he has managed to stay in power. As the first year ended, Yeltsin faced the challenge of his life—to remain in power and keep Russia moving down the path of reform. Commenting on his situation, Yeltsin said, "I have faith in our reforms. But if they fail, I can already feel the breath of the redshirts and the brownshirts on our necks."

7

The Impact of the Soviet Collapse

THE FALL OF the Soviet Union has had a tremendous impact on the rest of the globe. It is as if a great earthquake has taken place—its shock waves radiating out from the center to distant nations. The world is no longer divided into two enemy camps, and long-established divisions and alliances are disintegrating. Despite the hostility between East and West, the two sides had achieved a kind of balance of power that, in a way, created a stable political climate. Even though at times it seemed like a balance of terror, the different countries usually knew where they stood. But when the Soviet Union collapsed this climate became uncertain again.

Today, countries are trying to feel their way in this new environment. Alliances are being formed and shattered as friends become enemies and enemies become friends. No one knows for sure what is going to happen in the years to come. But one thing is certain—one era is over and a new one is beginning. And in this new era, it is likely that Russia and some of the other more

(Opposite page) East and West German leaders pose hand in hand after signing an agreement approving German reunification.

91

powerful post-Soviet states, like Ukraine, will play a significant role.

Forging new alliances

The absence of the East-West confrontation has left many countries free to renew old ties and, in some cases, forge new alliances. One area in which ties are being formed is Europe, which was divided by the Iron Curtain for nearly fifty years. The collapse of the Soviet Union has allowed former Communist-bloc countries in Eastern Europe to forge economic ties with the nations of Western Europe. For Western Europe, former Communist-bloc nations provide new markets in which to sell products. For the former Communist-bloc nations, Western Europe represents a doorway to modernization and economic progress. The countries of Western Europe long ago realized the benefits of allowing free trade between them. They formed the European Economic Community (EEC), also called the Common Market, to simplify free trade between member nations. Now, the EEC hopes to bring in the Eastern European nations and they, in turn, are eager to join.

Before the Eastern European countries can function equally within the EEC, however, they will have to set up capitalist economies. It will take an enormous effort by Western Europe, which will have to provide the bulk of the money and technology needed to accomplish this task.

Like Eastern and Western Europe, East Germany and West Germany have also renewed old ties. Germany has been divided since the end of World War II. After Eastern Europe broke free and the Soviet empire began to crumble, Communist East Germany and democratic West Germany seized the opportunity to become one country again. They officially reunited in October 1990.

Together, they face many challenges and problems that they did not face as separate nations. The new country faces serious financial problems as it tries to bring East Germany's failing communist economy into a capitalist one. And like the other satellites, East Germany inherited terrible environmental and health problems from the Soviet Union, which the newly reunited country has to handle. For the first two years alone, reunification cost the new German government $100 billion.

Another problem the new country faces is the rise of extreme German nationalism. Youth gangs are forming who shout Nazi slogans and harass—and even kill—foreigners. Fear is building among the majority who are not involved, yet the specter of Nazi Germany under Hitler has caused unease in the United States, France, and Great Britain. Despite the difficult times, however, the citizens of Germany today continue their efforts to meld the eastern and western sections of their land.

Rethinking old relationships

As a result of the fall of the Soviet Union, countries are not only forging new alliances, but

At a history-making ceremony in Rome in 1957, leaders of six Western European nations sign treaties establishing a common market, the first step toward European unity. Eastern European countries hope to join this economic union.

In a display of extreme German nationalism, East German skinheads raise their arms in the Nazi salute and shout Nazi slogans.

are rethinking old relationships. In the post-Soviet era, needs and goals once shared have changed, and some partnerships may have outlived their usefulness. One example is the relationship between the United States and Western Europe. In the wake of the Soviet collapse, the United States and Europe are reevaluating their relationship on defense issues. American troops have been stationed in Western Europe since World War II under the terms of the NATO alliance. NATO was designed to demonstrate that America and Western Europe stood united against any show of Soviet force toward Western Europe. When the Soviet Union fell and the Communist threat ended, however, NATO's stated military purpose also ceased to exist.

This has prompted much discussion among NATO members. Some believe the need for NATO has passed and that the organization should be dismantled. Others believe that NATO can be a positive force in unstable times but that its goals and objectives must first be revised.

Author Doug Bandow, who was a special assistant to former president Ronald Reagan, is among those who believe NATO has outlived its usefulness. "NATO was created four decades ago to protect war-ravaged Europe from Soviet domination," Bandow writes. But Soviet domination is no longer a threat. And now that this threat is gone, Bandow and others believe, NATO has no more work to do. "The lack of such a threat ends any pretense that NATO has a role in the future," Bandow writes. "It's time to send the American-led alliance into early retirement."

Former president Richard Nixon is among those who believe that America must maintain its involvement in NATO and that NATO has a role to play in maintaining a secure Europe. "Until a viable substitute evolves and proves itself, we would be making an irrevocable error in dismantling NATO or disengaging from NATO. In a period of massive instability in Eastern Europe and the Soviet Union, we should be exploring ways to preserve NATO rather than looking for ways to eliminate it."

Although the debate over NATO continues, NATO members have already taken steps to alter their relationships on defense matters. In 1990 NATO leaders agreed to reduce American troop strength in Western Europe. The United States has begun withdrawing its 350,000 soldiers.

Struggling on alone

When the Soviet Union was at the height of its power, it provided other Communist countries with trade and aid. The economies of some of these countries depended almost entirely on their relationship with the Soviet Union. Cuba was one such country and is now trying to struggle on alone. For more than thirty years, the Soviet Union supplied Communist Cuba with money, food, and weapons. Around 75 percent of Cuba's imports—and nearly all of its oil—came from the

Soviet Union. The Soviet Union stationed troops in Cuba to prevent the United States from trying to overthrow Castro. In return, Cuba provided sugar and other products to the Soviet Union.

Cuba's dependence on the Soviet Union was made stronger by the U.S. economic blockade of Cuba, which the U.S. established thirty years ago soon after Castro took over. The Soviet Union ignored the blockade but many other nations agreed to abide by it. Some agreed because they shared the U.S. desire to oust Castro and replace his Communist regime with a capitalist democracy. Others went along because they did not want to anger the United States.

The blockade created difficulties for Cuba but its economy remained healthy while it had its Eastern-bloc trading partners. This changed when Soviet trade with Cuba ended in 1991. The new post-Soviet states have not renewed any ties. The resulting drop in Soviet oil imports has caused a terrible energy shortage in Cuba. As a result, factories have closed, and many people have lost their jobs. On the streets, bicycles have replaced automobiles, while in the fields, oxen have taken the place of tractors. Cuba has tried to find other trading partners and foreign investors without much success. As a result, Cuba's economy and its people are struggling mightily just to survive.

The fall of the Soviet Union not only caused Cuba economic problems but indirectly triggered mounting unrest toward its government. Without the Soviet Union, Cuba is now much more alone politically. Castro is fighting the tide that swept away Communist governments in the Soviet Union and Eastern Europe. Set on keeping Cuba Communist, Castro has refused to make any reforms. This has deepened the suffering of the people already under stress economically, and increased the possibility of a revolt against Castro.

Violence and instability

The breakup of the Soviet Union not only caused economic desperation, but led to violence and instability in other Communist countries. Perhaps the most vivid example of this is Yugoslavia, which was Communist but not under direct Soviet control. In this country warring ethnic groups, which have hated each other for centuries, have torn apart the state and changed the face of Europe once again.

After World War II, Yugoslavia was set up as a multinational state, divided into six ethnic republics—Croatia, Slovenia, Bosnia-Herzegovina, Serbia, Montenegro, and Macedonia. Although each republic had a dominant ethnic group, the populations in these states were mixed. The people lived together peacefully because of the tight controls imposed by Yugoslavia's Communist government and because they feared unrest would encourage Moscow to impose direct rule on their country.

When the Soviet Union lifted controls in Eastern Europe and the satellites broke free, the Communist government of Yugoslavia collapsed too. Many of the country's ethnic groups seized their chance for freedom. Croatia and Slovenia declared their independence from Yugoslavia. Before long, only Serbia and Montenegro were left in Yugoslavia.

Under Serbian leader Slobodan Milosevic, Serbia began waging war on the breakaway republics. Milosevic said he wanted to protect Serb minorities living in those republics. He also wanted to form a Serbian state from the wreckage of Yugoslavia. In Milosevic's drive for a Serbian state, more than two million people have been pushed out of their homes, and more than 100,000 have died.

Western governments and the United Nations are trying to help but have been unable to stop the bloodshed. One official said, "Too many people,

Dazed refugees from the war-torn Yugoslavian city of Vukovar, site of a brutal three-month siege, debark from a convoy carrying 1,600 civilians.

too often and too fast, are prepared to resort to the use of the gun and the bayonet."

How should the world respond?

How the world responds to the fall of the Soviet Union will help determine what role the post-Soviet countries will play in the new era. These countries are struggling to handle the terrible problems they inherited from the Soviet Union. Of all of these problems, the economy is probably the most dangerous. The people, whose standard of living was not high under communism, are suffering terribly as most of these states try to set up capitalist economies and Western-style democracies. Success is by no means certain. Western nations have sent urgently needed food and medicine, but their governments are unsure of exactly how much and what kind of additional aid to provide.

Two brothers hold each other and weep during the funeral of a third brother, one of many Bosnians killed in ethnic fighting in the breakaway republics of Yugoslavia.

Many people in the United States and other Western democracies want to let these former enemies take care of their own problems. They feel that pouring money into the post-Soviet states is a waste because of the seriousness of their economic problems. Those who share this viewpoint also feel that many of the post-Soviet countries do not really want reform and are still dominated by communism. And they fear that Russia, the most powerful state to emerge from the wreckage of the Soviet Union, may become a threat to world security. So, instead of loans or outright aid, these people suggest that the United States and its allies in the West should establish trading ties with the post-Soviet countries and send advisers to teach these former Communist countries capitalist and democratic ways. In the United States, especially, there is a lot of resistance to spending money abroad when there are so many needs to be fulfilled at home. Nicholas Eberstadt, a researcher

from Harvard University, stated his view that aid to the post-Soviet states was a mistake:

> Foreign aid will not rescue Russia, because what ails Russia today is not merely a shortage of hard western cash. . . . What ails Russia is its legacy of communism. For over 70 years, the Soviet government . . . distorted the economy . . . through attacks on private property . . . command planning, and an unceasing war against the consumer. Russia may have awakened from this long nightmare, but it is still lying in its old bed.

Other people in the West believe that the post-Soviet countries not only need food and medicine, but hard cash to ease the suffering of the people and protect the gains made by democracy and capitalism. However, they favor not only direct cash payments, but also investing money in businesses in the former Soviet Union. They believe that if Western democracies do not send massive amounts of aid, Russia and the other post-Soviet states, which have no tradition of democracy, may return to dictatorship. In other words, saving dollars now may mean another cold war with Russia or another post-Soviet state. And the last one cost the American taxpayers five trillion dollars.

Michael Mandelbaum of the Council on Foreign Relations in New York City commented on the value of sending aid to the post-Soviet states:

> Economic deterioration leads to instability. If attempts at economic reform fail . . . you could . . . have a reconstituted, nasty Russia of the pre-Soviet period—the looming menace of the 16th to 19th centuries. If there is that kind of government, the Europeans won't be happy—and neither will we. The logic of economic aid is clear. This is a case of where an ounce of prevention is worth a pound of cure.

Who knows what the future will bring? It is only clear that, as one Russian poet said, "It is useless to break the wall of the future with your forehead and try to predict what is going to happen. There is a system even in the insanity of regimes, but only our successors will understand it."

Glossary

atheism: A belief that there is no God.

autocrats: Rulers with total power.

balance of power: When different sides or countries have about the same amount of power.

bipolarism: The domination of the world after World War II by two new superpowers—the United States and the Soviet Union.

black market: An illegal market where a wide variety of goods can be bought for generally very high prices.

capitalism: An economic system in which private citizens or companies own the means for producing goods.

cold war: A fifty-year period of hostility and tension with no actual fighting between the United States and the Soviet Union.

collective farm: A group of small farms merged to form larger ones under government ownership and control.

collectively: As a group.

commonwealth: A union of governments in which each country has control over its own affairs but works with other countries in areas of shared interest.

communism: An economic system in which there is no private property, and the people as a group own the means for producing all goods.

consumer goods: Products, like clothing and household goods, that people can buy.

conventional weapons: Non-nuclear weapons including guns, bombs, and tanks.

cooperative: Enterprise in which the workers own and operate the business and share the profits.

coup d'etat: Sudden revolt.

czars: Early Russian emperors.

democratize: Giving the people a voice in the government.

dissidents: Critics of government leaders and government policies.

entrepreneurs: Organizers of new businesses.

ethnic group: Group of people with the same history, language, religion, and customs.

federation: A union of individual states or republics.

glasnost: Mikhail Gorbachev's policy to encourage the people of the Soviet Union to speak their minds openly.

incentives: Rewards.

inflation: An increase in the amount of money and the resulting increase in prices.

joint ventures: When two parties or countries join together to form a business, sharing both the risks and the profits.

multinational state: A country that is made up of many nationalities or ethnic groups—a country of countries.

multiparty system: A system of government in which many different political parties are allowed to operate.

nationalism: A love of one's country and a desire to put its interests first.

perestroika: Mikhail Gorbachev's policy for restructuring the economy and the government of the Soviet Union.

planned economy: An economy in which the state makes all the economic decisions, including what and how much to produce.

price controls: When a government, such as the Soviet government, sets prices and keeps them artificially low.

privatize: Transferring businesses from government to private ownership.

satellites: Nations controlled by another country, such as the countries of Eastern Europe that were controlled by the Soviet Union.

secede: Withdraw from.

serfs: Peasants who were bound to their master's land and transferred with it when it passed to another owner.

shock therapy: Yeltsin's plan for rapidly setting up a market economy in Russia by lifting government price controls and privatizing all state-owned farms and factories.

socialism: An economic system that falls between capitalism and communism in which the government owns the means for producing goods.

sovereignty: Self-rule.

specialize: Produce one product.

state farm: A huge, state-owned farm that is run like a factory.

supply and demand: Supply is the amount of a product available, while demand is the amount of a product that people want to buy; together, they help set prices in a capitalist economy.

totalitarian state: A state with one leader who holds all the power and controls everything.

Suggestions for Further Reading

Joanne E. Bernstein, *Dmitry: A Young Soviet Immigrant*. New York: Clarion Books, 1981.

Wyatt Blassingame, *Joseph Stalin and Communist Russia*. Champaign, IL: Garrad Publishing, 1971.

Philip Clark, *The Russian Revolution*. New York: M. Cavendish, 1988.

Vincent V. DeSomma, *Union of Soviet Socialist Republics*. New York: Chelsea House, 1992.

Cecilia Fannon, *The Soviet Union*. Vero Beach, FL: Rourke, 1990.

Steve Feinstein, *Soviet Union in Pictures*. Minneapolis: Lerner Publications, 1989.

Anne Galicich, *Samantha Smith: A Journey for Peace*. Minneapolis: Dillon Press, 1987.

Stephen Goode, *The End of Detente: U.S.-Soviet Relations*. New York: Franklin Watts, 1981.

Kelvin Gosnell, *Belarus, Ukraine, and Moldova*. Brookfield, CT: Millbrook Press, 1992.

John Haney, *Vladimir Ilyich Lenin*. New York: Chelsea House, 1988.

Nigel Hawkes, *Glasnost and Perestroika*. Vero Beach, FL: Rourke, 1990.

W.A. Douglas Jackson, *Soviet Union in the Global Community*. Grand Rapids, MI: Gateway Press, 1988.

Karen Jacobsen, *The Soviet Union*. Chicago: Childrens Press, 1990.

Peter Otto Jacobsen and Preben Sejer Kristensen, *A Family in the U.S.S.R.* New York: Bookwright Press, 1986.

Robert A. Karlowich, *Young Defector.* New York: J. Messner, 1981.

Michael Kort, *Mikhail Gorbachev.* New York: Franklin Watts, 1990.

Keith Lye, *Take a Trip to Russia.* London: Franklin Watts, 1982.

Claire Rudolf Murphy, *Friendship Across Arctic Waters.* New York: Lodestar Books, 1991.

Laurie Nadel, *The Kremlin Coup.* Brookfield, CT: Millbrook Press, 1992.

Ina Navazelskis, *Leonid Brezhnev.* New York: Chelsea House, 1987.

Fred Newman, *Leaders of the Russian Revolution.* Morristown, NJ: Silver Burdett, 1981.

Walter Olesky, *Mikhail Gorbachev: A Leader for Soviet Change.* Chicago: Childrens Press, 1989.

Steve Otfinoski, *Mikhail Gorbachev: The Soviet Innovator.* New York: Ballantine Books, 1989.

John Pimlott, *The Cold War.* New York: Franklin Watts, 1981.

Abraham Resnick, *Lenin: Founder of the Soviet Union.* Chicago: Childrens Press, 1987.

James Riordan, *Soviet Union: The Land and Its People.* Morristown, NJ: Silver Burdett, 1986.

Elizabeth Roberts, *Georgia, Armenia, and Azerbaijan.* Brookfield, CT: Millbrook Press, 1992.

Stewart Ross, *The Russian Revolution.* New York: Bookwright Press, 1989.

Stewart Ross, *The U.S.S.R. Under Stalin.* New York: Bookwright Press, 1991.

E. Ryabko, *We Live in the Asian U.S.S.R.* New York: Bookwright Press, 1985.

E. Ryabko, *We Live in the European U.S.S.R.* New York: Bookwright Press, 1985.

R. Conrad Stein, *Invasion of Russia.* Chicago: Childrens Press, 1985.

Gail B. Stewart, *Soviet Union.* New York: Crestwood House, 1990.

George L. Vogt, *Nicholas II.* New York: Chelsea House, 1987.

Works Consulted

William G. Andrews, *The Land and People of the Soviet Union*. New York: HarperCollins, 1991.

James H. Billington, *Russia Transformed: Breakthrough to Hope*. New York: The Free Press, 1992.

James Cracraft, *The Soviet Union Today: An Interpretive Guide*. Chicago: University of Chicago Press, 1988.

Mikhail Gorbachev, *The August Coup: The Truth and the Lessons*. New York: HarperCollins, 1991.

Bernard Gwertzman, *The Collapse of Communism*. New York: Time-Life Books, 1991.

Geoffrey Hosking, *The Awakening of the Soviet Union*. Cambridge, MA: Harvard University Press, 1991.

Robert G. Kaiser, *Why Gorbachev Happened: His Triumphs and His Failure*. New York: Simon & Schuster, 1991.

Vladislav Krasnov, *Russia Beyond Communism: A Chronicle of National Rebirth*. Boulder, CO: Westview Press, 1991.

Walter Laqueur, *The Long Road to Freedom: Russia and Glasnost*. New York: Charles Scribner's Sons, 1989.

Walter Laqueur, *Soviet Union 2000: Reform or Revolution?* New York: St. Martin's Press, 1990.

Stuart H. Loory and Ann Imse, *Seven Days That Shook the World: The Collapse of Soviet Communism*. Atlanta, GA: Turner Publishing, 1991.

Richard Lourie, *Russia Speaks: An Oral History from the Revolution to the Present*. New York: Edward Burlingame Books, 1991.

Robin Milner-Gulland, *Cultural Atlas of Russia and the Soviet Union.* New York: Facts On File, 1989.

Yuri Ovsianikov, *Invitation to Russia.* New York: Rizzoli, 1990.

Susan Richards, *Epics of Everyday Life: Encounters in a Changing Russia.* New York: Penguin Books, 1990.

Eduard Shevardnadze, *The Future Belongs to Freedom.* New York: The Free Press, 1991.

M. Welsey Shoemaker, *The Soviet Union and Eastern Europe 1990.* Washington, DC: Styker-Post Publications, 1990.

Andrei Sinyavsky, *Soviet Civilization: A Cultural History.* New York: Arcade Publishing, 1988.

Hedrick Smith, *The New Russians.* New York: Avon Books, 1991.

Anatoly Sobchak, *For a New Russia.* New York: The Free Press, 1992.

The Soviet Union. Amsterdam: Time-Life Books, 1984.

The Soviet Union, Second Edition. Washington, DC: Congressional Quarterly, 1986.

David and Peter Turnley, *Moments of Revolution: Eastern Europe.* New York: Stewart, Tabori & Chang, 1990.

Raymond E. Zickel, *Soviet Union: A Country Study.* Federal Research Division, Library of Congress, 1991.

Index

About the Author

Brenda J. Smith is an author and editor, specializing in elementary and secondary social studies education. During the last fifteen years, Ms. Smith has contributed to a variety of social studies textbooks and ancillary programs, many of which were completed during her lengthy tenure as an editor for the Merrill Publishing Company. After receiving her bachelor of arts degree in history and government from Ohio University in Athens, Ohio, Ms. Smith completed graduate coursework there in American and European history. A former teacher, Ms. Smith is a member of the National Council for the Social Studies and the Ohio Council for the Social Studies.

Picture Credits

Photo research by Susan Friedman, San Francisco, CA.

Cover photo by The Bettmann Archive
AP/Wide World Photos, 8, 9, 17, 29, 30, 33, 36, 38, 42, 43, 47, 50, 53, 54, 55, 58, 67, 70, 73, 76, 78, 80, 82, 83, 87, 98
The Bettmann Archive, 6, 10, 12, 14, 15, 20, 24, 39
ITAR-TASS/SOVFOTO, 27, 32, 64, 71
Library of Congress, 26
North Wind Picture Archives, 16
Reuters/Bettmann Newsphotos, 45, 48, 59, 62, 74, 85, 90, 94, 99
RIA-NOVOSTI/SOVFOTO, 19
SOVFOTO, 18, 22, 44
TASS from Sovfoto, 13, 46, 56, 69
UPI/Bettmann Newsphotos, 25, 31, 93